D.I.Y. Home Improvement Manual

Master Basic D.I.Y. Projects

Jackson Bennett

Table of Contents

"You can't just sit there and wait for people to give you that golden dream. You've got to get out there and make it happen for yourself."

Diana Ross

A Special Gift to Our Readers

Our DIY Checklist is included with the purchase of this book. The following checklist will assist you in preparing for the new DIY projects.

Please let us know which email address to deliver it to by visiting our website at www.jackson-bennett.com

Introduction

If you own a house, you know that there is always work to be done around your home. There's always some project that needs to be finished. Perhaps you have found yourself in the middle of a bathroom renovation project and regret not scheduling it early enough. You find yourself hammered by tile issues. A two-week renovation has turned into a six-week endeavor, and just when you think you've finished it, it's time to start over.

When renovating their house, a couple found what every homeowner wishes for—a suitcase. The two top floors of the house had just been renovated, so they were finally able to make it down to the basement. Upon discovery, they took the green case outside and laid it on the grass. Initially, the husband thought it was baseball cards. But, when they opened it, there were three wrapped packages inside. They were filled with joy as they found the packages all loaded with money. One package had 20-dollar bills, and the last two were 50 and 100-dollar bills—over $23,000 in total, and many of which dated back to the late 1920s and 1930s. According to the couple, they believe the bag was stashed in the 1950s because it was lined with newspaper from that time.

Home improvements do not guarantee you a windfall of money; however, the next time you remodel your home, consider doing it yourself to save some money. The cost of upkeep does not have to drain your bank account. In most cases, you can do a project, like working on a steel door, for a tenth of the cost of hiring someone else to do it. Home improvements are just as satisfying as building a house from scratch.

The Doorstep to Handiwork

The prospect of remodeling your home can be both exciting and intimidating. Home improvements increase the overall value of a property, while also making it easier for you to realize your dream home. To ease the burden of this task, I've gathered a few DIY home improvement tips to help make your home more beautiful and functional. The information in this book will show you exactly how to accomplish that—whether you're a beginner or a seasoned pro.

Perhaps you have lived in the same house for years, and have now decided it's time for an upgrade. Or, you've purchased an older home that needs a lot of care to reach its full potential. Old homes are good fixer-uppers. However, renovations seldom go smoothly as with any home improvement project, a renovation involves meticulous planning and effort. Homes can deteriorate over time, and once the renovation begins, it is very common to find that previously unknown problems are lurking beneath the old wallpaper. There is no need to be concerned if you don't have a passion for working with tools, but you do have a passion for preserving your home's beauty. Learn to take good care of your own home by using the love that you have for it.

Handiwork has been a passion of mine since I was a child. Many people would like to make their own design decisions based on their own set of tastes and preferences. Interior design is inspired by many things and places. Although a few of the tasks of your reno may be straightforward, choosing a layout or color scheme can bring out your creative side. Changing your home's white bulbs to calming yellow ones can immediately improve the ambiance. Make sure your new bulbs are LEDs so that they will last for a long time. Plants and flowers are among the most effective ways to update bland, dated spaces. The simplest potted plants freshen the air and add a sense of well-being to any room.

Outside of my work, I've had the opportunity of helping my friends and family with some home improvements. I always made sure to leave them with a few tricks for future handiwork. Although hidden problems can arise in any renovation project, they should never stop you from taking the steps to renovate your home. Knowing what to look for and what to expect is half the battle when it comes to common renovation issues. To help you with your renovation project, I'd like to talk about the most common issues we encounter and how to deal with them.

Whenever I'd get house calls, I'd always be responding to do some findings on why a water electric bill was high. This is why I believe that the most important home improvements include your water and lights, as well as the ambiance of your home. Homeowners often have to deal with water damage because it is such a serious problem. Leaks in the roof can sometimes lead to water seeping into the ceiling before they are noticed. A broken or leaking pipe can also cause water damage. Whatever the cause, the effects can be severe, from rotten wood to mold. Perhaps you are considering updating your light fixtures and recently purchased a new washing machine. The demand placed on modern appliances may be too much for old electrical wiring, especially if you are improving an old home. The worst that could happen is a fire. Whatever you do, it is best to bring it up to current standards.

The smallest changes to your home can make the biggest difference. Find out how easy it is to enhance your home by tackling one of these DIY home improvement projects.

CHAPTER 1:

Staying Informed and Prepared

DIY projects keep your home lively and interesting, as well as provide you with a sense of purpose. They are also a great way to stay active and motivated. Simply walking up and down the stairs a few times can provide you with a cardio workout. You can add weight resistance by carrying heavy objects while you do this.

Learning new skills helps you maintain an active and healthy brain. Now and then, you should challenge yourself by doing something you have not done before, and DIY is a great way to do that. While it might be easy to just buy what is in style when decorating your home, it is much better to create a look all your own. DIY projects are never quite the same for two people. You will be able to make something unique with your hands.

Cutting Costs

Renovations are quite expensive. Even the unexpected leaking tap can cost a few dollars or so. While some people may prefer opening a credit card or borrowing money from friends, opening a dedicated account will give you a better idea of your savings progress and prevent you from taking money out of your savings. Spending less each month can help you cut costs in preparation for big projects. Home projects can often be handled more cheaply when you do them yourself.

You can save a lot by reusing or repurposing fixtures and materials. Salvaged materials can also be found at places like Home Depot for a fraction of the cost. Some contractors may be wary of working with salvaged items, or homeowner-supplied materials in general, because they may be held responsible if something goes wrong. Therefore, by fixing up your house yourself, you have control over what items are purchased and at what price. While your creativity may be flowing while decorating your home, it is important not to overdo it. Many homeowners get carried away. Prioritize the changes that you need to make in each room, and then build gradually. Focus on the major changes, then the minor fixtures can follow later.

There are many other reasons that one should like to pursue the DIY route. Many people have earned money with DIY, it's not just about saving money. Thousands of DIYers are sharing their creations and techniques on YouTube and their blogs, and they are getting lots of visitors. We all know that if you catch a lot of attention, you can make lots of money.

Professional Work

While preparing for a renovation, one of the biggest questions is whether to perform the work yourself or hire a professional. You should avoid DIY projects that, if performed incorrectly, may cause real problems, like a leaky pipe in the wall that can cause water damage or faulty electrical work that can cause a fire. If you are planning to sell your house, you want to make sure it is in the best shape possible. DIY projects done by amateurs can turn away potential buyers. It is even possible that they wonder if there are other problems with the property. Experts who work in homes daily know what it takes to get excellent results. Tiles can be laid easily by DIYers, but the floor and the walls will never be perfectly level. They always have imperfections or bumps.

While a professional might figure it out, a homeowner may struggle with it, affecting the installation and how the tile ends up looking. Some projects don't need professionals. You can do a lot of cheap and easy home improvement projects to save money. You can, for instance, install fixtures to prevent the clogging of your drains. Savings on plumbing costs would be substantial. Also, you can consider simple upgrades to make your home more energy-efficient like changing the light bulbs.

Rather than painting your entire house at once, paint one room at a time and evaluate the time commitment, skill required, and results. Consider taking on projects that are reasonably achievable in one day and that you will be able to complete with the tools you already own. Don't jump into projects that involve permits, plumbing, electrical work, or structure changes. It is common to do some aspects of remodeling or upgrading yourself as well as working with a professional. In a project such as a bathroom remodel, you may decide to take on the role of a general contractor. However, you may want to hire subcontractors for specialized work, such as electrical wiring, plumbing, and cabinet installation.

DIY Law

As required by law, homeowners should ensure that any new building plans or renovations are approved by the local authority before starting the project. It is important to get approval for any changes that you might make to your property, including building a wall around your property, installing a swimming pool, or a second story. Extending walls and adding on to a room will certainly increase interior space, but there are also some other creative options. As long as removing internal walls does not affect a building's structural integrity, they can be removed without obtaining planning approval. You must ensure that the wall you're tampering with is not a load-bearing wall. To be on the safe side, it is best to double-check with your local authority concerning the requirements for making such alterations.

It is not necessary to have a permit from the municipality for a relatively minor renovation, such as replacing flooring or countertops, but major renovations usually require one. Among this list are any home additions, changes to the heating and cooling systems, interior plumbing, and electrical systems. When it comes to changing the garden or paving in an estate, you may have to consult your estate council. Most estates maintain uniformity in their appearance, so you may not be able to select different wall colors. Even though you may own land, you can't do whatever you want with it. You can access property records at any time. Online searches can inform you of zoning laws and allowable structures on a property. You could face hefty fines if you fail to obtain the necessary permits for a home renovation.

It is important to factor permits into your budget, as well as your timeline. Even if you are only renovating or adding to an existing house, always include time and costs for permits. People see getting all of these permits and following the requirements as tedious, but the best builders, architects, designers, or contractors wouldn't miss these crucial steps. Whether you do it yourself or hire a contractor, make sure you are informed, educated, and compliant before you begin, otherwise, your project may end up having to be altered or even completely removed. Build smartly by researching.

Tools to Begin

When it comes to DIY projects or home maintenance, half the fun is choosing the right tools. As you undertake various DIY projects, your tool kit will evolve. There are some things that power tools are great for, but they are also a luxury. A great deal of work can be done using only hand tools.

Screwdrivers

Screwdrivers are versatile tools that can be used for tightening cabinet hardware, installing light switches, and cracking open metal paint cans.

Measuring Tape

This can make measuring everything from the wall area for painting to the thickness of wood at the home center very easy.

Hammer

You can use the curved claw to remove bent nails. A hammer is used for general construction, framing, nail pulling, cabinet making, furniture assembling, and upholstering.

Duct Tape

Due to its multipurpose nature, duct tape is now used for sealing, repairing, packing boxes, and other purposes.

Flashlight

You won't have to worry about searching for fresh batteries whenever the breaker trips or whenever you need to work inside a dark sink cabinet.

Pliers

Among many things you can use them for, you can straighten bent power cord plugs, install new showerheads, slice cables, and generally grip things well.

Adjustable Wrench

The wrench is essential for tightening and assembling all types of appliances and swing sets.

Painting Tools

Paintbrushes, rollers, paint trays, and roller handle extensions are all necessary supplies for DIY painters.

Toolbox

It's easier to stay organized and more convenient if you keep all your drivers, screws, and bolts in a toolbox.

Be sure to keep yourself safe when using these tools. Safety gear that you need to always have with you includes:

- A pair of safety glasses

- Protective hearing devices

- Masks for respiratory protection

- A pair of work gloves

- Wear hard hats

- Knee and ankle pads

- First Aid Kit

- Fire extinguisher

- A pair of work boots

It is said that purchasing hand tools will save you money. You will not be required to pay a technician for any repairs needed around the house. Small repairs, such as loose door hinges and broken kitchen cabinets, can be easily done.

Time Management

You should approach your DIY project as if it were a journey. Before you can figure out how to get to your destination, you need to know what you want. Take in all the necessary information about the project you are working on by reading and watching renovation TV shows. If you know someone who has done this before, you could get some practical advice directly from them. Doing your research saves you time in that you won't have to redo any mistakes.

After you have finished your research, you should make a list of all the things you are going to need. If you need to purchase some items, purchase them all at once, instead of stopping midway which will affect your work time. List everything you want to do.

List the materials, prices, quality, stock availability, the skills and expertise of the DIY crew if they are needed, and any other necessary information. Additionally, make a list of all of the helpful reminders and cautions you have gathered, so you will not forget them while working on the DIY project.

DIY should be broken down into stages and parts. Thus, you'll know exactly what to do first and by what deadline. Additionally, dividing a project into stages complies with budgeting principles. In cases where money is tight, it helps you to determine which materials and items are most important. It's also important not to waste too much time trying to make everything perfect.

Foresight is required to estimate how long a project will take. Simple projects often are grossly underestimated and cause frustration. It is particularly frustrating when you realize you aren't even halfway through the project when you should have met the deadline. A rainy day contingency plan should also be considered in case you cannot begin painting your exterior wall on those days. Also, include other projects in your schedule that you could perform in place of the rainy days.

Learning the Basics

Most people avoid DIY projects out of fear of doing them wrong. It's easy to learn DIY and grow your skills if you're eager. You should start small if you are a beginner. Repair a few nagging appliance problems, put up a shelf, or remove the old radiator fluid. You can build your confidence once you've mastered the small tasks. Sharing your knowledge with your friends, family, or loved ones is an excellent way to learn. By doing so, you can review what you already know and maybe even come up with new ideas. There are some DIY ideas you can try including fixing minor plumbing issues, cleaning and inspecting gutters, and repairing your air conditioner.

Construction

A home is built long before the foundation is laid. A plan and a competent builder are essential to a successful construction process. Budgeting is one way to avoid costly construction mistakes. Take caution when banks offer you more money than you can afford. The house project should not cost the maximum amount you can get from the bank. Keep your expenses as low as possible. You can determine how much you can afford to spend on a house by speaking with an independent financial advisor. You should also compare the prices of several contractors before settling on one.

The best way to build your own home is to hire a general contractor who is licensed. Homeowners can often act as their contractors in many states. This arrangement often leads to you being referred to as an owner-builder. If you are going to hire a contractor for a large-scale project like a house rather than a shed or a small, lower-cost structure, it will be necessary for you to submit an owner-builder exemption application. This means that the work on your property is your responsibility.

Most people don't have the skills necessary to be their general contractors. Building a home involves pulling together many strands and ensuring that they are coordinated in countless ways. There must be a proper sequence of projects and sub-contractors, interrupted by numerous inspections by the city. A good understanding of the building code is necessary. Additionally, having a network of reliable subcontractors is immensely helpful. General contractors are responsible for all of that. Home construction is not something that can be done cheaply. Generally, general contractors charge 10-to-20 percent of the total cost of the home, including permits and materials. Especially if they have previous experience in general contracting, it's a fee that most beginners find well worth paying.

You can participate in your house build by doing smaller, individual projects. These projects related to the late stages of the contract may be undertaken by homeowners rather than by contractors:

- Designing and building patios and walkways

- Adding trees, shrubs, and grass to the landscape

- Painting the exterior of the house

- The installation of window treatments

- Laying carpet

- Completing the basement

DIY projects at this late stage are ideal because you avoid the risk of slowing down the construction process.

Electric

When you don't know how to handle electronic components you can have a difficult time handling electronics for any practical application. Knowing how the power works in your house can help you better manage power use when working on home renovations. To avoid power trips, you will know to switch off power demanding devices.

Electric meters: Power is supplied to your home by your electric meter and your power service provider. Service cables run from the utility company's meter base to your house. You can measure the amount of electricity consumed in your home by using the meter.

Disconnect switch: Some homes have a dedicated disconnect switch attached to an outside wall near the electric meter. Disconnect switches allow you to shut off the power from outside the house in the event of a fire or flash flood, or if you need to repair the system. This saves you from having to enter the house to turn off the power.

Service panel: The electrical service passes through the meter and into the main service panel, commonly called the breaker box, of your home. All the heat from inside the service panel is connected to two large hot wires, called lugs, which are mounted on the service panel. In between the two service wires is the neutral bus bar, which has the purpose of providing a neutral connection. The hot wires carry the electricity to the house. The electrical circuit is completed after the electricity flows through the household system and is then brought back to the utility via the neutral wire.

Circuit breaker: All of the branch circuit breakers in the panel are disconnected when the main breaker is turned off, as are all the circuits in the house. When the main breakers are off, power still flows to the main panel and service lugs unless a separate disconnect switch is engaged.

Branch circuit breakers: All the devices and appliances on a circuit are shut off with the turn of a breaker. Overloads or faults cause the breaker to trip. You've probably overloaded the circuit if you're using a high-demand appliance, like a vacuum or heater. By placing the appliance on a different circuit, you can then turn the breaker back on.

Devices: Light fixtures and appliances all connect to electricity as devices. Each device is connected to a branch circuit that begins at the main service panel.

Switches: Lighting and fans are controlled by switches in the house. By flipping off a switch, you are breaking the circuit. As soon as the switch is switched on, the circuit is "closed," allowing power to flow to the device.

Outlets: Among the devices that can be plugged into an outlet are televisions, lights, computers, vacuum cleaners, freezers, and toasters. The outlets in the average home provide between 15 amps and 20 amps of electricity; a 20-amp outlet can provide more power without tripping a breaker. A high-demand appliance such as an electric range or clothes dryer may require a special outlet providing 30 to 50 amps or more. In potentially wet areas of the house, such as in bathrooms, kitchens, and laundry rooms, it is mandatory to install GFCI (ground-fault circuit interrupter) outlets.

Wiring: Several types of wiring are used in a home, including non-metallic cables, Bx cables, and wiring seated in conduits. Circuit wiring is usually done with NM cable. It can be used in dry areas. In the case of dishwashers and garbage disposals, Bx cable is frequently used where the wiring of the appliance is visible. The wiring inside of conduit is designed to be protected from exposure in garages, sheds, and outdoor applications.

When working with electricity, it's important to remember that water conducts electricity. Even a little contact could be dangerous. Ensure that any spills are wiped up to avoid getting water on the plugs. It is a good idea for parents to cover any unused electrical outlets with tamper-proof caps. Children should be kept away from cords that are hanging loosely.

Plumbing

All of us decide whether a certain job can be done by ourselves or if we need a professional. Check out how to shut off your house's water. Your property can be badly damaged by a burst pipe or a similar plumbing emergency. Getting the water turned off faster will lessen the extent of the damage. It is common for homes to have a valve in the garage.

You should fix your leaking faucet if it leaks. Replacing the washer will usually fix leaky faucets. If the faucet is loose at the base, tighten it with a wrench first. Replace the washer inside the faucet if that doesn't work.

There are ways to stop your toilet from running continuously. The flapper inside the tank usually doesn't close properly, causing a running toilet. The shut-off valve for the toilet is located behind the bowl on the pipe. You might need to adjust the chain if it's broken or not long enough.

It is possible to unclog a plugged toilet. In case of a blocked toilet, you should always keep a plunger nearby. Make sure the level of water inside the toilet has been lowered as much as possible before using the plunger. Many drain problems can be resolved with drain cleaning chemicals. For a more natural approach, pour baking soda into the drain, then vinegar, and then boil water. Taking hair out of a drain may be necessary to clear clogs. You can save a lot of money by learning basic plumbing skills.

Outdoor and Garden Work

Getting a garden started is like buying real estate. It depends on the location. Ideally, you should plant your garden in a place where you'll be able to see it frequently. This will increase your chances of spending time in the area. You should always plan your new garden around access to water. Install a hose, so that you won't have to carry water to the garden site all the time. Before deciding where to put your garden, consider how the sunlight will affect it. Most plants, such as vegetables, herbs, and fruits, need at least six hours of sunlight to thrive. Starting a garden requires fertile and well-drained soil, which is one of the top pieces of advice.

Various plants can also be grown from pots, including mushrooms, vegetables, herbs, flowers, and fruit trees as well as trees, bushes, and berries. Use a pot that is large enough when gardening in containers. It is important to choose plants that are adapted to your growing conditions. Sun-loving plants should be placed in a sunny section, heat-tolerant plants should be used in warm climates, and vines such as pumpkins and melons should have ample space. Some plants can be bought as seeds, while other vegetables are available as seedlings.

CHAPTER 2:

Decoration and Upkeep

Interior design is a fun and creative activity that also helps you keep things organized and controlled, staying ahead of any maintenance or upkeep issues. It also helps you stay ahead of any potential maintenance issues and keeps you involved in knowing what's going on around your house. It is no secret that interior design greatly affects the way we feel and think. Certain colors are considered relaxing in interior design, compared to other colors that give us energy instead. Similarly, the amount of light we let into our house can also affect our mood. Did you know that including windows in your home decor can be extremely effective in alleviating pain and discomfort?

Interior design trends vary greatly depending on the culture, customs, and beliefs of a country, as well as what items or materials are available in their country. Interior design encompasses various specialties such as structural design, design for business, computer technology, handwork, aesthetics, and more. The combination of these specialties reflects the sphere of interior design and its breadth. As is the case with odd numbers in general, three is a magic number in design. Cushions, vases, and pictures in odd-number arrangements add visual interest to the arrangement that can't be achieved with even-number arrangements. Together, these elements will enhance a room's aesthetics and increase its functionality as well. What is currently trending in interior design is only a small part of what it is. Interior design might seem like an area we are familiar with - picking the right color carpet, setting the location of candles, and putting lighting in the right place, but there are so many other aspects we don't know about interior design that can benefit us.

Decorating isn't the only aspect of interior design. The decoration is only a part of what you do. Maybe you've thought interior designers arrange your couches and hang pretty drapes and paintings. The colorful part comes after all the hard work. It comes after the calculating and measuring, the mixing and matching. Every detail of the house must be considered when doing interior design. Everything from the electrics to the plumbing, to the lighting, to the ergonomics, and the proper use of space. Considering how the house is built or influencing structural changes when doing renovations. Design is part of the plan and not an afterthought.

Color Choices

When it comes to painting your house, don't be afraid to put some thought into the color choices. Colors can influence how we feel. Colors like red increase appetite, which is why most restaurants use red in their branding. Blues and greens are nature-like and relaxing. Purple is popular with children, but not necessarily with adults. Yellow is cheerful. It is beneficial to use yellow in rooms where homework will be done, but avoid it in bedrooms, as these are usually reserved for relaxing. You can sleep better by choosing calming colors for the bedroom.

You can use warm colors for social areas like dining rooms, kitchens, family rooms, living rooms. Opt for cool colors for private areas like your home offices, powder rooms, and bedrooms.

Matching Colors

Looking at the bottom of your color sample card is a good place to begin if you're unsure which color to choose at the paint store.

Make a color palette by choosing three colors from an existing item in your house. If you have an object that conveys comfort or has an emotional connection to you, such as a favorite pillow from the family room sofa, a tie or scarf, or a painting, take that object to a paint store. Since each sample strip typically contains six colors, if you find three strips that contain those colors, you'll have 15 to 18 options to choose from. Next, you should choose one color to paint the walls and save the other two to use in fabric or furniture around the room. Take the same three color samples you took for the first room and pick a color for each adjacent room. Decide on a fourth color you can use as an accent. Add a touch of color to every room of your home with a cushion, plate, or artwork in the shade. In this way, the spaces in your house are connected.

Warm and Neutral Colors

Rooms can be made elegant and flexible by using neutral colors. Colors such as white and beige are no longer considered neutral. Changing the color of a simple living room and adding redaccents to the trim can make it look elegant.

It's easy to keep a neutral room chic by combining cool gray with warm tones like honey. While the overall effect of this design is restful, the contrast between the two opposites awakens the otherwise sleepy room. Gray is today's hottest neutral for your home's decor.

Gray offers the appearance of both warmth and cool depending on its chameleon-like nature.

Coloring Your Walls

If you don't want to decorate four walls in the same hue, consider how you want the final product to look. A bold accent wall or molding in contrasting color are both excellent ideas.

Preparation

An effective paint job starts with scraping, sanding, patching, and filling every crack, hole, and imperfection on the surface. If you are painting over dark colors or new drywall, you must prime the walls and ceilings first. The primer stops strains from seeping through, it allows you to only paint one coat and reduces peeling and blisters.

How to Hold the Brush

1. Dip the brush in the paint directly up to 1/3 or so of the length.

2. The brush should be lightly tapped against both sides of the can or jug. By doing this, the brush is loaded with more paint.

3. Paint should not be scraped off the brush by dragging across the bucket edge. By doing that, you simply remove the paint, compress the bristles, and render the brush useless.

4. Cut along the corners of the ceiling from left to right if you are right-handed. Those who are left-handed should paint from right to left. The paint will flow better if you can see it flowing.

5. Hold the brush in the same way you would hold a pencil and gently press the bristles against the wall.

6. When painting an area with two colors, you should begin with the lighter shade and allow it to extend slightly over the adjacent shade.

7. With the paintbrush held at about 45 degrees, paint several diagonal strokes across the area.

8. Distribute the paint on the large flat area with horizontal strokes of the paintbrush.

9. If you want to use a freshly loaded brush, you should not let the paint dry completely. You will get visible lap marks from doing so.

10. After each stroke, raise the paintbrush off the surface. In this way, the paint stroke is feathered.

Pattern Painting Wall Ideas

Stenciling is an easy and simple method for adding sophistication to a wall. It's as easy as ordering the stencil you desire and spending an afternoon painting your walls. A harlequin pattern can instantly bring life and movement to the interior design of any room, whether it's the kitchen or nursery. In addition, you can use black and white stripes, polka dots, checkerboards, and sponging styles.

Unless you have more work to do tomorrow, you won't have to clean your paint brushes and paint-roller sleeves after finishing the day's painting. You can brush off the excess paint and wrap them in plastic food wrap.

Changing Wallpapers

You can learn how to remove wallpaper from your walls if you're ready for a fresh start. You will need to remove the old wallpaper whether you are painting or re-papering. It's a straightforward DIY project that you can complete in one day and you don't have to hire an expert to do it.

Preparing Your Wall

Organize the room by removing anything from the walls and placing things in the center. Ensure that the remaining furniture and floors are protected from getting wet with drop cloths. Make sure the electricity has been turned off, and tape all outlets and light switches.

Before you begin peeling your walls, make sure they're plaster or drywall. It is possible to damage drywall if it's too wet. It's also necessary to know what type of wallpaper you'll be using. A Putty knife can be used to loosen a corner of the paper so that it can be peeled away. Strippable wallpaper comes off easily. You have peelable wallpaper if it peels apart but the backing remains.

Taking Down Strippable Wallpaper

A Putty knife is needed to lift the corner of the paper. You should loosen another corner of the paper if the paper rips. Do the same thing around the room. As soon as you have taken down all the paper, wipe the walls with soap and water to eliminate any residue. Paint the walls only after they have dried completely.

Removing Traditional Wallpaper

Strip wallpaper with hot water and wallpaper stripper. Fill up a spray bottle or use a garden sprayer to apply the solution. Spray the solution in a small area of the wall with the spray bottle. After several minutes, let the solution soak in. Remove the wallpaper by peeling it off using a putty knife. It may be necessary to score the wall or apply the solution before scraping the wallpaper if the solution does not absorb.

Applying Wallpaper to the Wall

Before you begin, gather the tools you will need:

- A roller for painting

- Straightedge

- Paper roller

- Wallpaper smoother

- Measuring tape

- Knife taping

- Chalk line

- Level

- Utility knife

- A pair of scissors

- Sponge

If you are going to install wallpaper, make sure you have enough. Start by removing the light fixtures and plate covers. To prevent having to wait for it to dry before applying another layer, fill all holes with a non-shrinking joint compound. Using a drywall knife or sandpaper, remove small imperfections from the walls. Use a primer to cover the entire wall. Using a roller, apply the paste. The first run must overlap to ensure plumpness. To create an even overlap, start from the inside corner of the wall and leave at least one-eighth inch between the wallpaper and the adjacent wall. If you hang the paper this way, you will always have a plumb corner regardless of how well the corner is situated.

Lay the paper so that when you unfold it, you will be working with about two-thirds of the panel. Use a smoother to go over each square inch of paper. Avoid stretching the paper or squeezing out the paste too hard. After hanging the sheets, you should clean each off with a natural sponge. Rather than waiting until the paste dries up to clean it up, it's significantly easier to do so while it is still moist. The edges can be set with a roller. Pressing too hard may cause too much adhesive to be squeezed out. Cut through the middle of the overlap. Take one panel and fold it over the other. Then, cut the overlap down the middle. The knife blade should be angled so that more of the blade is cutting than just the tip. For cut guides, if your hand cannot hold a steady position, take an ordinary drywall knife. When cutting wood trim and other objects, use scissors instead of a knife.

It is normal for air to get trapped between your paper and walls when you install it. Once the paper has settled and the adhesive has dried, the air will be gone. You can poke a small hole in it with a pin and gently press it out with a wallpaper sweep if it does not.

Hanging Items

Art does not have to be the most expensive to be perfect. For a piece to be truly meaningful to you, it must complement the space where it is placed as well as forge a deep emotional connection.

Choosing a Place to Hang the Items

Before choosing a picture to hang on a wall, ensure that you check its size before having it printed and framed, or framed only if you have chosen a piece of fine art. The general rule is to pick a larger piece of art for your living area or behind your bed. The weight of your artwork should also be kept in mind. A heavy piece of art will require stronger nails. Your artwork should also be spaced evenly. A piece of art should be separated from another so it doesn't appear cluttered if it is attached to the same wall. Rooms with too many pieces and insufficient spaces appear smaller.

In general, pictures should be hung at eye level. A good place for the midpoint of the picture is generally between 57 and 60 inches from the ground depending on the height of the ceiling. Picture frames should never be placed in direct sunlight because they will become permanently damaged.

Hang Paintings and Photo Frames

If you're going to hang a picture that is heavy on a plaster wall, you should find a stud where you can secure the wall hook. There are, however, a variety of options for anchoring wall hooks into plaster walls if you do not have a stud near the place you want to hang your picture. One option is to use hollow wall anchors, while another is to use toggles that expandand spread the pressure.

Adhesive hooks can hold lightweight pictures. In addition, adhesives that cannot damage the paint are available here as well. Brick walls can be drilled with a masonry bit, a plastic wall plug, or some expansion spaghetti hammered in, and then the screw lodged in. If your paneling is wood, you can secure it with a nail, screw, or picture hook. A flush mount wall hanging kit is ideal for hanging something flush against the wall, such as a canvas, or picture frame. If you've decided on how to hang your painting, determine whether you'll use picture wire or a metal hook attached to the frame.

Creative Curtain Ideas

Curtains fall part of the design of your home. By hanging your curtains high, you'll appear to have high ceilings. Consider hanging your curtains closer to the ceiling if you feel your apartment is a little cave-like. There will be an instant illusion of higher ceilings.

Types of Curtains

Sheers: In general, sheers are mostly transparent and do not provide a lot of privacy. However, they also have a beautiful flow due to their lightness. They also cast an ethereal light throughout a room because they let so much light through.

Window Scarves: Framed in a billowy style, these are mostly decorative and can be used as stand-alone pieces or layered with traditional curtains for a more elaborate look.

Semi-Sheers: Though more private than sheers, semi-sheers still allow for plenty of light to pass through, making them ideal for communal rooms or use as over shades in bedrooms and bathrooms.

Blackouts: The use of blackout curtains is self-explanatory as they provide greater levels of comfort and privacy. The fabric has a liner that makes it opaque and thick.

Hanging Your Curtains

Step 1. Gather the following items before hanging curtains:

- Step ladder

- A pair of safety glasses

- Measuring tape

- Pencil

- Level

- Bits and drills

- Stud finder

- Anchors for the wall

- Curtains

- Hardware for curtain rods

Step 2. Take measurements.

Make sure to measure your windows before getting curtains and rods. If your window is eight to twelve inches wide, add eight to twelve inches to determine the rod length. Window treatments should be wide enough for each curtain panel. You should measure the curtains from the top of the rod to the floor. Make the drapes longer if you wish them to pool.

Step 3. Install the brackets.

Mark your drill holes with a pencil. You should place each bracket approximately four to six inches from the sides of the window frame. The entire window treatment will look crooked if your pencil marks are not level. Ensure that your brackets are aligned with the studs with a stud finder.

Step 4. Install the curtains and rods.

To remove creases and wrinkles from new curtains, iron or steam them. Thread the curtain onto the curtain rod after removing the finials. You may need to replace the finial before putting the rod into the bracket depending on the type of bracket. Once you have installed the rod, you will want to tighten the set screws that hold it in place.

Carpets For Your House

A rug can make a huge impact on the look and feel of a home. You can use them to link a whole room, have a designated reading or play area. Depending on the room, carpet tiles might work well in an office or a playroom, while a luxurious carpet might work well in a guest room. Carpets are also not suitable for every home. Older homes may have carpets in the bathroom, but this can cause a problem because it is a bathing area. The toilet and bathtub are much better places to use carpeting sparingly. A carpet can also serve a functional purpose and not just be decorative.

Laying Carpet to Fit Your Room

If you plan to install carpet over a concrete subfloor, you can use masonry tacks or epoxy adhesive to fix the tackle strips. Install the carpet pad perpendicular to the carpet installation direction, and then staple it with a staple hammer near the tackless strips. You will need to feel through the padding to identify the strip, and you will then need to use a utility knife to remove the padding around the edge. If you can, stretch out the carpet on both sides and notch the back.

The carpet should be rolled outward with its back facing outward until the notch areas are visible. Make a chalk line extending between the notches. Open the door to the room and roll out the carpet. Straighten it out as best you can. The extra carpet should be cut, but leave three inches on either side of the walls.

You need to sew the carpet edges where they meet. To keep both carpet segments straight, the seam edges must be straight. Put one end of the carpet against a wall. Carpets can be trimmed around obstacles by using a carpet knife.

The knee kicker should be used to attach the carpet to the tackless strips. With a wall trimmer, you can cleanly trim excess carpet at the correct location by resting against the wall. To attach the strips on the other side of the room, use the power stretcher. Any area where the carpet does not abut a wall, such as a threshold, should have a binder bar attached. Then cut out the vent openings once the carpet is all in place. Consider attaching shoe molding to a room if you wish.

Decoration and Design Ideas

When thinking of the style of your home, you can use already existing features of your house to create a look.

Master Bedroom

A black-and-white bedroom can feel boring unless it is filled with textures and patterns. The natural tones in this bedroom, along with accessories such as triangle pillows and rug, further enhance its style. Your room can also be adorned with nature. The sky peering through the windows of this room makes it look like an art piece.

Kid's Bedroom

Focus on what your little one loves most to create the perfect room for them: playing! You can also add large toy features, like a tall giraffe that reaches the ceiling or a huge elephant in the room. Designing a child's bedroom can be fun and you can never go wrong with exaggerating your style. This will be amusing for your kids.

The Office

It may not be possible for you to have an office at home. If that is the case, you should maximize your vertical space. Small spaces require a lot of organization. Hanging file folders, shelf holders, rods with hooks, and even wall-mounted systems let you organize office supplies while keeping them close by. Consider a standing or sitting desk if you work long hours.

Living Room

By installing a fireplace as a focal point for your living room, you can make your living room look warm and bold. Use colors and textures to your advantage. You can design your living room for beach living if you know you live near the beach. Adding a huge hanging swing and a collection of colorful paintings to your house can make a statement. Self-portraits and family portraits are also good choices.

Dining Room

It is important to understand the purpose of space before designing it, as well as the purpose it will serve. Does space have enough space for a formal dinner party as well as for casual gatherings? Is the space better suited for intimate discussions or group discussions? You can then plan your space and choose materials and furniture based on the answers you provided. Guests can converse easily and comfortably at small round tables. Having long, narrow rectangular tables maximizes the number of guests along the perimeter, but the conversation patterns are very different.

The Kitchen

Kitchen cabinets can be easily and inexpensively updated by painting them. It isn't feasible to upgrade to a high-end Smeg refrigerator, yet you want to give your fridge or freezer a fresh look, then try this fridge hack: attach leftover wallpaper by double-stacking it to the front of the appliance.

CHAPTER 3:

Ceilings and Walls

Home maintenance schedules are essential for maintaining a house. You can prevent breakdowns, save money, and keep your home looking its best by checking your appliances, heating and cooling systems, plumbing, and electrical systems.

Start With the Walls

A wall can be either load-bearing or non-load-bearing. Load-bearing walls support the weight from above, typically another floor or roof. Walls that are not load-bearing are built independently from the house's main structure.

An exterior wall is usually thicker than an interior one. The interior walls are not usually responsible for supporting roof weight, so they can be thinner; the interior walls also play a lesser role in insulating the building against heat and cold. A desert-like climate requires thicker walls, whereas tropical climates require thin walls.

External Walls and Internal Walls

Insulation applied to solid walls inside a property is almost identical to the type applied to external walls, except that there is no insulation applied to the exterior. External insulation is the best option. External has the advantage of not being limited by space. When installed internally, a room will obviously shrink, but if done externally, there is no change. Insulation on your exterior walls keeps damp from penetrating the walls—the exterior render applied to your wall top critically creates a barrier and prevents the passage of water.

Blocking Up a Doorway

When blocking up a doorway, it is important to remove the door and hinges. Your wall won't be as strong if you block off the door without first removing the door frame. In between each row, stack cinder blocks with frame ties. Cinder Blocks are inexpensive, lightweight, and strong. Stack the bottom row of blocks, and then screw the frame ties onto the walls just above. Then, stack a second row on top of that. You will need to stack your blocks and add frame ties between each layer, so that the surrounding wall will also hold them in place.

Plaster the block wall on both sides with a hand tool and spread the plaster over the wall in a circular motion. After applying the first layer of skim plaster, allow it to dry. The second layer should be thick enough to match the surrounding wall. Let the plaster fully harden and dry.

Stud Partition Wall

Partition walls can be used to create smaller bedrooms, and, in some cases, bathrooms. Structural studs do not support any loads.

Building and Fixing

As a rule of thumb, always measure twice and cut once. On your partition wall, you must first cut the top and bottom plates. To build top and bottom plates, always use lumber that is longer than 12 or 16 feet. You should place them parallel to each other and perpendicular to the wall. As you position and screw in the top plate, someone may need to assist you. Be sure to always use the proper anchors when securing the plates.

Anchors vary according to the type of wall. When buying anchors and screws, always pay close attention to the type of wall. The ground plate must be measured twice and cannot run through the doorway. Having cut your top and floor plates, mark where you want your studs to be distributed. 16-inch centers are the most common, but 24-inch centers can also be used. Screw-in the studs starting at the two ends. Consider the door when measuring the studs for the wall if you plan to install one. Using a preassembled door frame is another option.

Door placement can be done anywhere on the wall, but studs at either end of the wall provide more support. As soon as the studs are attached, you may measure and nail the noggins into place to fit between the studs. If extra support is needed, add another notch every four or five inches horizontally along with the studs.

Metal-Stud Partition Walls

Metal-frame stud wall kits can be an easier and cleaner alternative to traditional stud walls if you need to partition a room with no sound issues. Compared to a normal stud wall, the finished wall will be about 75 mm thick and much lighter, so it will be less likely to overload the floor.

Tiled Ceilings and Walls

You can replace an existing ceiling by installing ceiling tiles on it.

Choosing Tiles

Tiles of small sizes are usually used in residential spaces such as bathrooms, kitchens, and toilets. A room feels more spacious and airy when it has large tiles. Wall tiles can be used on the floors, but floor tiles cannot be used on the walls. Matte or polished finishes are up to personal preference. Glazed tiles have a smooth surface, whereas terracotta tiles have no glaze and require sealing to prevent staining.

Setting Out Wall Tiles

Tiles should be laid out according to certain principles:

- Place the tiles in such a way that equal-width tiles are on both sides of a horizontal feature, such as a window.

- If you have a bath or worktop, make sure that you have full tile height above.

- Whenever a recess is deeper than one tile, have the front edge of the recess covered with a full-size tile.

- It is best to avoid using narrow strips of tiles near corners and at the top and bottom of walls.

- Patterned tiles can be used around corners.

- Whenever you use patterned tiles in a layout, make sure they are evenly spaced.

- Do not try to tile around objects, like basins and electrical outlets. Remove the item and tile behind it, then reinstall it. A far better finish appearance is obtained by doing this instead of attempting to get it done through more difficult means.

Fixing Ceramic Tiles

An error many DIYers make in tiling is spreading adhesive too smoothly. Apply the adhesive horizontally with your trowel or older fork. Flattening the ridges will help you gain grip, as well as level the surface. Tile spacers are excellent for ensuring even tile placement. There are many different types of spacers you can use. You can use plastic spacers or cardboard or matchsticks.

Unless you have a tile cutter, make sure you leave 24 hours between laying tiles and grouting them, so that the adhesive is fully set. Utilize a squeegee to evenly spread the tile grout, and work slowly while covering a small area at a time. Before the grout dries, remove it so that a long cleanup will not be necessary.

Fixing Broken Tiles

When a broken tile is on the floor, it can cause tripping hazards and makes your home look unattractive. Tiles that have cracks or chips are easily repaired by painting them. Apply a thin layer of tile filler to the cracked area, mixing it with the matching paint color. You can wipe it down with a damp cloth once it has dried. Use a clear coat to give your finish a glossy appearance. Using a contrasting paint color, create a new, colorful design.

Laying Ceramic Tiles

In most cases, choosing tiles for walls comes down to personal preference. As opposed to on a floor, such places do not have to pay attention to technical parameters. It is more important to pay attention to the size, color, and design of the tiles. A tiled wall creates a visually interesting surface. Several colors and patterns can be arranged to create an aesthetic effect.

Quarry Tiles

There should not be any voids underneath a quarry tile bed for the load to be properly transferred to the foundation. Be sure not to end up with very narrow tiles along any wall by calculating the number of tiles necessary and designing the layout. Hand-made tiles should be soaked in water for several hours before you use them. Work from the center outward, covering the area with mortar with a flat mason's trowel tipped with a notched section. Cover approximately nine tiles at a time. Start with the center intersection and continue working towards the walls, pressing the tiles into the mortar firmly.

These tiles are perfect for utility rooms and other places requiring hard-wearing surfaces. Unlike ceramic tiles, they are usually unglazed, thicker, and are usually installed with mortar and mortar rather than adhesives. Due to its high slip resistance, quarry tiles are ideal for areas where people must walk without slipping. As well as being extremely durable, it provides excellent traffic resistance.

Working on Your Roof

It is not safe or comfortable to be on a roof. Protect yourself from slipping by wearing shoes with rubber soles. Work with a buddy and wear a harness.

Pitched Roofs

Most homes with flat roofs are too small to drain water efficiently, especially in rainy areas. Homeowners in states with heavy snowfall are at risk of being snowed in. Pitch roofs prevent water accumulation.

Pitched Roof Coverings

The cheapest way to cover a pitched roof is to use interlocking concrete tiles. Due to their size and the fact that they do not require much overlap, only ten can be used on a square meter, making them extremely quick to lay.

Maintaining a Pitched Roof

A pitched roof is usually covered in slates. The best way to ensure the integrity of a pitched roof is to leave the job to professionals who use the right equipment. Most people choose chemical cleaners. The old way of scrubbing slates was not only inefficient and labor-intensive, but it also shortened the lifespan of the slates because of wear and tear. Taking a visual inspection of the roof quarterly will help prevent moss, algae, and damage.

Flat Roofs

Many homeowners choose flat roofs these days. They are not only highly durable but pretty easy to maintain. Regular inspections of flat roofs will help prevent the need for repairs. Maintain your roof by scheduling an inspection every two to three years and calling in a professional if anything goes wrong. To determine whether the heat of summer or the cold of winter has damaged your property, an inspection should be carried out in early autumn and early spring. If your roof needs an inspection, look for clogged gutters, missing roof shingles, damaged drainage, and any signs of decay or rot.

Flashing

Flashing is usually installed around roof features, such as vents and chimneys. Flashings should direct water down the side, instead of into the roof deck, so that it runs straight into the shingles. Flashing seals can be renewed by removing old mortar and caulking along edges. The flashing and chimney joints should be sealed with masonry caulk. A urethane roofing cement or silicone caulking compound should be used for sealing the seam between the cap and step flashing. Aluminum, copper, and steel are usually used to make roof flashings, which prevent water from accumulating below shingles. Flashing is essential to prevent leaks.

Guttering

A gutter should be inspected twice a year, every autumn and spring.

Maintain your gutters as follows:

1. Make sure your gutters are clean by checking them regularly and removing any leaves and other debris.

2. If your gutters are sagging or slipping, use gutter screws, which are attached with a cordless drill. Compared to gutter spikes, gutter screws provide much more support and security.

3. Make sure no leaks are present at the joints and seams by using a hose. A leaky joint can be repaired by cleaning the area thoroughly and applying silicone caulk.

4. Inspect downspouts for debris and ensure that any joints fit properly.

5. You should ensure that the water coming out of drains is channeled away from the home by splash blocks, downspout extensions, or irrigation pipes.

Home Window Repair

The safety and visual quality of a window are important factors when determining whether it should be replaced. You can repair single-pane windows yourself or have a glazier do it for you.

Repairing and Replacing Windows

Window repairs are necessary for the following situations:

- Broken or cracked glass (replace the sash)

- A single-pane window with a broken mullion or muntin

- Sliding windows that move slowly or are stuck

- The cap on the exterior of the drip tray is missing or damaged

- Windows with poor casings

- Minor leaks of water

What to consider when replacing your windows:

- A foggy window with condensation inside

- Faux muntins/mullions of poor quality on the interior

- Problems with the structure

- A major water leak has occurred

Interior Shutters

You can preserve a shutter's beauty and functionality for many years by maintaining it. Shutters are made from various materials, including vinyl, aluminum, and wood. No matter what materials they are made from, you can use a clean, soft cloth to dust them.

In wet weather, wood may become discolored. Wood shutters are best cleaned with a duster or soft cloth dampened with furniture polish. You should wipe the wood dry immediately if it gets wet. A mild detergent can be used to clean aluminum, faux wood, and vinyl shutters. Clean and oil exterior shutter hinges once a month if you live in an area that has excessive pollution, dust, and dirt. With a few drops of household lubricant, stiff and squeaky hinges can be easily fixed.

Types of Glass

Glass is now the most popular material for decor construction, as sustainability and durability are highly desired. Glass was used mainly for its visual appeal, but now it is the most popular material for exterior and interior architectural structures. The ceiling-to-roof windows are often used in many modern homes to bring light and views into every room. When choosing window walls as part of your architectural structure for your home, it is best to go with tempered glass.

Toughened Safety Glass

Tempered glass is also known as toughened safety glass, it can be used for a selection of purposes like shower doors, tables, shelves, and furniture, and is far less likely to break. When broken, it splinters into small granules rather than sharp shards. There are fewer chances of injury from the granular chunks. It is ideal as a glazing option for window walls.

Flat Glass

The flat glass comes from the float process, but it is not the main product. Glass of this type is commonly found in home windows. It is often used where transparency is not needed, such as in the bathroom, home or office door, or between teller counters in a bank. In addition, flat glass absorbs sound and protects against the sun.

Mirror Glass

A mirror is simply a plain sheet of glass, and mirrors come in all sizes from bathroom mirrors to full-length wardrobe doors. Adding mirrors in a room can visually expand the space and create a sense of brightness. You instantly add depth to a room when you mount a mirror to the wall. Oversized mirrors are popular for creating dramatic effects.

Repairing Broken Glass

To replace the old glass on a vinyl window, pry the vinyl stop off with a putty knife. Aluminum windows are held together by a metal strip and a rubber gasket. To remove the glass, you must remove both the metal strip and rubber gasket. Changing the glass in a vinyl window requires a bead of silicone; replacing the rubber gasket in a metal window requires cleaning.

Roof Windows

Instead of climbing a ladder to reach your high windows, use a window cleaning kit that extends. These can be simple mops mounted on poles, or more deluxe with built-in water tanks and triggers for squirting soapy water when needed. You can also purchase window cleaning accessories, like jet power washers and window vacuums that remove water, leaving a streak-free finish.

The Cleaning Process

First, dust the window so that there are no cobwebs, then sponge hot soapy water on the surface. You can use a specialty cleaning solution for windows or dishwashing detergent, which is effective for most surfaces. To catch drips, lay down a groundsheet beneath the window. An effective way to dry off and buff the glass is with a lint-free cloth.

Fitting Curtain Rails and Poles

You should check to make sure your ceiling and window head is level. In cases where they are out of level, rather than putting the poles in level it is sometimes better to raise them so they follow the ceiling line. Find the center of the window by measuring it. Using the measuring tape, mark the spot where the curtains should end and where the brackets should be placed. To ensure the curtain covers the entire window, mark the edge of the pole where it will overlap the window. Drill holes at the positions marked by your brackets. The brackets can then be screwed into the pot and curtain rings can be inserted into the pole. You can then hang your curtains after putting the curtain ring in.

Hanging Blinds

How do you cover your windows if you don't want to drill any holes in your walls or frames right now, or if you live in an apartment building that prevents you from drilling here or there? A temporary shade is a great solution! I have found that they are very inexpensive, low-maintenance, and easy to install. You just cut the strips to fit, peel off the protector strip, and stick them up. They don't look bad at all. If you are looking to change the design of your home by adding either black or white blinds, temporary shades are a good idea. It's also not damaging to the surface underneath when you take them down.

Door Plans and Ideas

Entry doors should be durable enough to withstand wind, rain, and intruders, yet attractive enough so that they make a good first impression. Most older doors have wood that warps and cracks over time. Similarly, some older steel doors have a peeling surface.

Replacing Front Doors

Replacing a door can sometimes be as simple as changing one slab of wood for another. Some older doors may require you to replace their framing, including the door jambs and threshold, particularly if the wood has begun to rot.

Even though the door frame itself is in fine condition, its studs can bow and settle out of the square. As a result, opening and closing the door is difficult. When fitting a new wood door into a misaligned frame, you'll have to plane both the top and bottom or even trim an edge to make it hang correctly. A wood door is the only one that can be planed or cut; metal and fiberglass doors cannot.

If you do not want to replace the entire frame, you can use door-replacement kits. A steel frame attaches to the old door, making it easier to hang the new door. In addition to the ease of installation, a steel frame adds security. However, these kits are only available in a few sizes, they are slightly smaller than the original opening, and they cannot be used to cover damaged jambs.

Whenever security and durability are top priorities, a steel door is the right choice. Compared to wood and fiberglass doors, steel doors will not crack or warp.

Fixing a Loose Door Handle

A Phillips screwdriver (crosshead type) and a flat-head screwdriver are all you need to fix your loose door handle.

You probably have a cover plate on your door handle. You can gently prise off the plate if the plate has been damaged. To do this, all you have to do is tighten the screws under the cover plate with a cross-headed screwdriver. They might need to be tightened in three or four places.

Maintaining Your Garage Doors

Regular maintenance and good observation skills can prevent garage door emergencies. You can inspect your garage door setup once a month by simply walking around. Be sure that there are no frayed or loose springs or hinges. Look for wood or paint deterioration on the exterior of the garage door. When you hear your garage door rolling in and out, listen for any reverberations that may have occurred. It is important to know where the fault lies if you notice something isn't right. You should contact an affordable garage door specialist as soon as possible if your garage door is malfunctioning.

Whenever possible, have your garage door serviced and lubricated once every six months. You should grease and oil parts like hinges and springs, as well as clean the tracks.

Benefits of Fire-Resistant Doors

The ratings of fire-rated doors vary according to how long they can withstand the heat and prevent the fire from spreading. Fire-rated doors can withstand heat for up to 20 minutes. A common misconception about fire-rated doors is that they can't be made of wood. The reality is different. Wood can be used to manufacture fire-rated doors, but the wood used to manufacture such fire-rated doors is treated with substances that allow the wood to withstand heat.

Installing a Fire-Rated Door

The most important thing is not just to select the best fire-rated door, but to install it correctly. The materials, sizes, shapes, and parts of a fire door all differ from one another. Fire departments approve fire-rated doors for specific situations and only professionals with the appropriate experience can install them in such a way that the door performs the way it is intended.

CHAPTER 4:

Everything Water

The plumbing system of a house, even the smallest one, appears to be often complex and confusing. When you make the effort to learn how a residential plumbing system works, you will understand that it's quite simple.

Two significant parts of the system exist, this is the incoming water supply system and the drain-waste system for removing wastewater.

Understanding How the System Works

Freshwater is provided by a system of pipes that enters the home. Pressure plays a major role in the system. These pipes carry water from the city or wells.

Normally, your house is connected to the city water main by a humongous pipe. If your link to the main isn't working, contact a professional. A main that gets damaged may lead to civil litigation and hefty fines. Water is usually obtained from wells by people without access to city water. A high-pressure pump then pumps water into the home. A low level of pressure prevents water from reaching the highest and furthest points in your house.

The earliest signs of low pressure are usually running showers and faucets. Pressure is affected by several factors, including leaks and blockages. It's relatively easy to resolve the leak if the root cause is a loose connection. The leak, however, may demand you to re-plumb your entire home. Plumbing is another task you should leave to a professional. Water is delivered to your meter through the main pipe. The shutoff valve is located before or after your meter. The water supply is cut off by the valve, making it useful when repairing the system.

Understanding your drain-waste-vent (DWV) system will help you if you need plumbing repairs at your home. Water drainage from your house goes to the sewer system, either through a city sewer line or a private sewer system, called a septic tank and field.

Various appliances, sinks, showers, and tubs collect water in the drain pipes. Water and waste material are removed from the toilet by waste pipes. Vent pipes let air into the system to ensure that wastewater flows smoothly. As the water flows down the drain, it fills a P-trap with water to prevent sewer gases and odors from entering the house. More water gets pumped through this water to keep it fresh.

A P-trap is attached to a drainpipe that enters an opening in the wall. The sewage system is managed by a soil stack behind the wall that is accessed by a vent line and drainpipe. Sewage is transported to the soil stack by drain pipes, and through the stack, sewer gases are transported to the roof by vent lines. A house's faucets, pipes, and vents are all part of the same draining, piping, and venting system.

Pipework: Types of Pipes

Various types of pipes are available, some made from classic materials, others more modern. Your home's plumbing can make a big difference in the way you live, so you want to make an informed decision when it comes to selecting pipes for your house.

Rigid Copper Pipe

Copper pipe is typically used in water supply lines inside the house. This is great for a water supply because it does not come with any health risks.

PEX Pipe

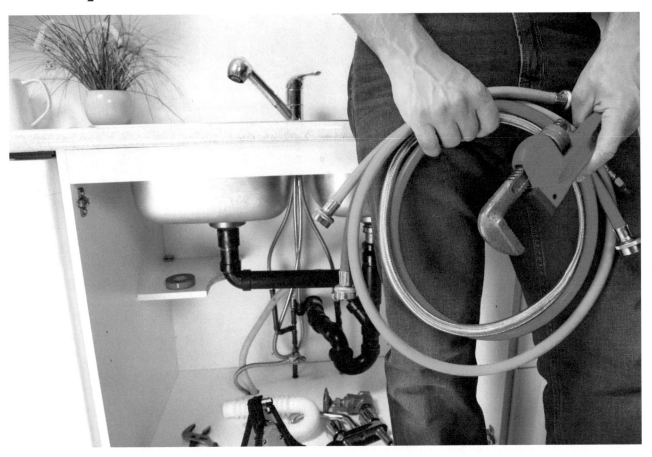

The only purpose of PEX is to provide water. It is a rigid pipe that can endure the pressure of water, but it is also a flexible tube that can be weaved around walls, ceilings, basements, and crawl spaces.

PVC Pipe

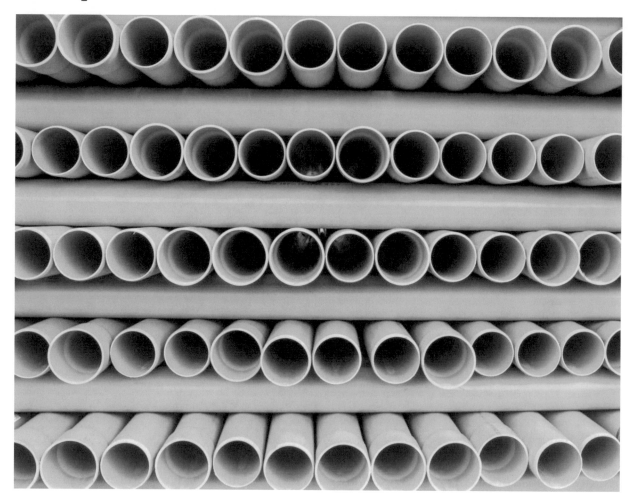

Pipes made of PVC are used as drain or vent lines in plumbing. At first, PVC pipe was popular because of its lightweight properties and ease of handling. PVC pipe can be easily installed and can be cut with little more than a hacksaw and a miter box.

Fitting Pipes

Pipes can be reused in different ways to improve aesthetics and functionality in your home, without requiring any plumbing. Laundry rooms often include plumbing-pipe clothing racks. You can install pipe flanges in studs and hang the racks on the wall for a closet from nowhere. Starting small is a good way to appreciate industrial design elements but without having to tear down the drywall and exposed pipes. You can create a pencil holder by cutting a copper pipe into equal pieces and hot gluing them together. Copper pipe is also good for creating a magazine holder and for hanging clothes.

This restaurant incorporated pipes into its ceiling in a creative way. It's a good idea for every DIYer to recycle pipes to create other uses.

Pipework can be difficult to purge of water. To begin with, you need to locate the drain point below the pipe you wish to solder. When water runs horizontally for a long distance, there can be a build-up of water in the pipe. If the pipe cannot be lifted, you can either attach a hose to the end and blow the water out, or, if you cannot move it, you can lift it slightly. Put gloves on as the flux can sting even a small cut. Brush flux onto the outside of the pipe after cleaning it. It is common for plumbers to apply some flux on the inside of the fitting, but this can cause flux deposits to form inside the pipe, which can eventually cause leaks.

Place your heat mat over any nearby surfaces to protect them from the pipe after it has been cleaned and fluxed. Set the flame of your blow torch to a steady, comfortable intensity. The fitting should be gently heated. When the flame is hot enough, touch the end of the solder wire to the fitting. It should melt the solder around the fitting when it is hot enough. On a 15mm pipe, one inch of melted wire is usually enough to create a watertight seal. Be careful not to burn your finger since the torch nozzle will be extremely hot. Use a mirror to inspect the joint. A thin solder ring should be visible around the fitting. Use a moist rag to clean the old flux off a pipe. If the fitting is water-tight, wait until it has cooled.

Concealing Pipework

Today, exposed plumbing is considered to be a feature. Rather than modern and minimally designed rooms, this works well in rustic or country homes.

The pipes can be hidden with a bookshelf if they are running vertically down a nook. You can build it yourself from floor to ceiling and create a cavity within the shelving to accommodate pipes without taking up any extra space. You could paint or cover them in cloth designed in the shape of candy canes if you are working in a girl's bedroom.

To conceal the items in the laundry room or bathroom, you can build some custom cabinetry. You can use this space to store cleaning supplies. Another inexpensive option is to get some fabric and sew a sink skirt using it.

Water Storage Tanks

Consider how you will use your tank before you install it. Would you use the water for rainwater harvesting, lawn watering, washing machine watering, and swimming pool watering?

Installing Water Tanks

Once you know how you plan to use the water tank, it can be installed very easily.

Step 1: Create the Tank Base

There are two types of water storage tank bases you can build. Material that is compacted and concrete:

1. **Concrete Base**

The concrete slab must be three inches thick and level on all sides. It must also be larger than the base of the vertical tank. Concrete must be poured after the earth has been adequately compacted.

2. **Compacted Material**

Compact a layer of crusher road base about 3 inches thick and 24inches larger in diameter than the water tank. The base of the tank must be free of any stones or sharp objects that could damage the tank. It must be compacted thoroughly and be perfectly flat and level all around. A retaining wall must be built around the base to prevent erosion due to washout or vermin.

Step 2: Install Overflow Drainage Pipes

A piping connection should be made from the fitting to the stormwater drainage system, or to a point well clear of the tank where the pipe will not damage the foundation.

Step 3: Install the Roof Fill Pipes

You can connect the roof of your tank to the lid with a pipe. Please discuss what filters you will need with your local dealer if you are using the water in your tank for human consumption. Your water tank's lid should also have your filter basket attached.

Maintaining the Water Storage Tanks

Normally, you would need a hose and pump to remove the dirty water from your rainwater tank. You can empty and sweep the rainwater out of your tank if the tank is large enough for you to get in. It can be dangerous to climb into a tank, so be careful. You can clean your tank's interior using a mixture of hot water and detergent. It can be done with an electric brush or a high-pressure water jet. Cleaning the tank without getting into it might be possible with a brush attached to a long pole. Water tanks should be cleaned at least once per year.

Many people do not know how to keep their water tanks clean, so they do not regularly clean them. Water can become contaminated with sludge or sediment over time.

Working With Taps

Two of the most common tap types are mixers and separate hot and cold taps. It is also possible to purchase the spout separately, or as part of a set, including the tap.

Choosing Taps

You can mix hot and cold water with one lever mixer tap. A lever on the side enables you to set the desired temperature. As a result of the fact that they are mounted on the wall, mixer taps are called wall-mounted taps. When replacing mixer taps, it is usually necessary to reinstall tiles that have to be removed for accessibility.

Separate hot and cold taps provide separate handles that control the temperature of the water through separate spouts. These tap assemblies are called wall top assemblies because the plumbing fittings are mounted on the wall and tiled surrounding. Since the fittings can be accessed more easily, they can be easily replaced. If you plan to replace taps, check the size of the hole in the tile behind the existing taps-you will want to make sure the new taps you select will cover that hole.

Installing New Taps

When you start a new project, you should have already installed your plumbing. You want to be certain it reaches the bathtub or basin properly.

You should insert your taps and washers into the holes in the bath or sink so that the washers are between the tap and the surface of the bath or basin. You will need to tighten a backnut to attach the tap. Once the taps are installed, the supply pipes may be connected. To do this, copper piping can be used or plastic push-fit fittings. For awkward placement, copper is useful, but you'll need a blowtorch to connect the lengths.

To connect to the water supply, tighten each end by hand until it feels like it will run smoothly. Try to maintain a clean plumbing system. Make sure that both ends are tight once you are done. Start the water and gently run the taps. Make sure that no water is escaping from the tap or the connections themselves.

Repairing Leaking Taps

Start by disconnecting the water supply at the tap. The tap handle must be removed. This is typically accomplished by removing the screw from the cover and lifting it. Turn the tap mechanism in an anti-clockwise direction to uninstall it. By doing so, you will be able to reach the tap washer at the bottom.

Removing the old tap washer is the next step. You will need to replace your washer with the correct size in your kit. There may be a small screw that needs to be removed. It is important to check the condition of the tap seat before re-inserting the tap mechanism. The tap seat of a leaking tap can be damaged or dirty, causing debris to accumulate. Buying an entirely new tap isn't necessary. Purchasing a tap resealing tool is all that's needed. With this tool, you can work on any taps in your house and save yourself some money.

Drainage

Whether your yard was never graded properly or over time it eroded or settled, there are ways you can make your grass look healthy again with no soggy or muddy spots. You can let your lawn bounce back to life with a yard drainage system that moves the water out of packed soil areas.

Creating a Drainage System

Find the spots on your lawn where water is retaining too much after rain. After completing each wet area, walk out in two directions and mark the location of the drainage hole. Put a rock in the spot to mark it. You should place the holes at a distance of three to six feet from the center of the wet areas.

At the drainage locations, dig a hole that is one foot wide and three feet deep. The sod should be removed before digging the hole. Remove about two inches of grassroots, as well as some soil, to ensure they survive when you put them back in place.

The surface grass should be removed starting in the center of the wet areas and proceeding toward the drainage holes. Set the line at one foot wide. The procedure should be repeated for each wet area. Excavate a trench 10 inches deep along each line. To drain the wet area, scoop more soil from the trenches. The slope should decline by 1/4 inch every four feet. Use a level to measure your progress.

Add a two-inch layer of gravel and sand to the trenches' bottoms. Water can easily flow through these two materials. By filling in some of the larger gaps, the sand prevents soil from spreading over the surface. Make sure that holes are at the bottom of the trenches when using perforated pipes. Cover the pipes with mesh sleeves to prevent sand, soil, and small debris from clogging the holes. Put gravel and sand mix along the pipe's sides and on top. Make sure the material clears the pipe by two inches.

Two inches of sand over the gravel will raise the trenches to surface level. Put the sod back on top of the sand. Pour the gravel and sand mix into the drains until the sand reaches the top of the trench. After that, the grass can be laid back.

Clearing Blockages

Every household has a plunger somewhere in the bathroom. It is important to use a cup-shaped plunger and not one with a flange. If the bathroom stopper is not currently in place, remove any metal strainers from the sink. In this way, a tight seal can be achieved with the plunger. The clog should be removed with sharp, fast movements, and you should check periodically to see if the solution has worked.

Make sure the plunger covers the entire drain. Then, pull and press quickly for about 30 seconds. To speed up draining, add more water to the drain before plunging. A rapid drain of water indicates you're on the right track.

Showers and Baths

It's important to know whether your water pressure is usually low or high. If you don't have high water pressure, you can boost it. When it comes to choosing what type of shower you need, water pressure plays a big role, purely because it determines how powerful your shower accessories will be. Your neighbors are a good place to start. If your neighbors' water pressure is good, you may need to call the water company to check the shutoff valve. However, if their pressure is also low you can install a booster pump.

It is important to get information about your water pressure, whether your water comes from mixer showers or digital showers, from your local council before you make any major changes. All your hot and cold water pressure will depend on the type of water system you have installed.

Electric Showers

It is perfectly feasible to provide hot water on demand when using an electric shower. Cold water is channeled directly into the unit from your mains system, then this water is heated.

Installing an Electric Shower

Using a chinagraph pencil, mark the position of the holes on the shower unit. A masonry bit should be used to drill holes. Unless the tile bit is ceramic, use masking tape or a tile bit if you're drilling into tiles. Install wall plugs and seal them with silicone.

Once you have infiltrated the pipe into the shower unit, connect the electric cable and screw it to the wall with the supplied screws. A connection can now be made between the showerhead and the inlet pipe. Tie the compression fitting firmly with a pipe wrench. Using the cable as a guide, connect the live, neutral, and earth cores to the load and earth terminals.

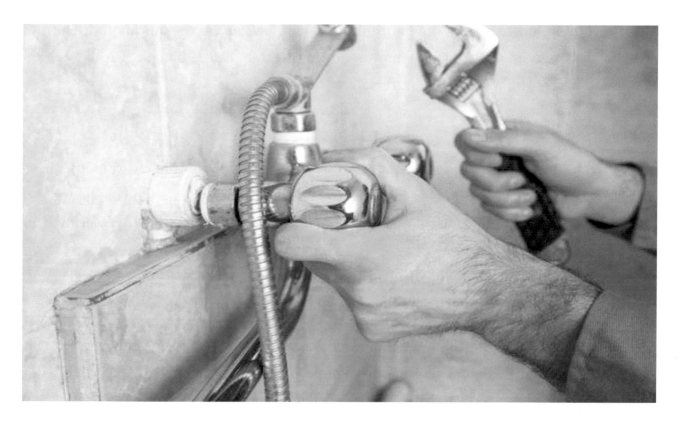

Place the rubber seal on the cover. You can now mount the rail after the unit has been plugged in. After that, connect the handset to the shower unit and the other end to the hose, then position it in the holder. Before using the electric shower, be sure it is working properly.

Mixer Showers

They are easily fitted into the designs of most types of bathrooms and shower enclosures, and they are compatible with high and low-pressure water systems.

Installing a Mixer Shower

Ensure all parts of the content are included. You should carefully cover the valve openings before you start installing the mixer so that no debris can enter when you're working on the supply pipeline. Be sure the shower valve is suitable for the wall type and that it is mounted properly.

Once you have decided on the location of the shower and the direction of the pipe entry, install the pipework leading to it. It is important to secure the cold and hot water pipes to the wall or panel for stability and to prevent movement after installation. You should always install compression olives and flush the pipework before connecting to the shower valve. Test the water for leaks by turning it on.

Power Showers

The power shower is a popular choice among those who enjoy relaxing techniques since it features specialized jets for massaging the body. A Part P certified plumber must install an electric shower, so that all wiring is located correctly. If you choose to install an electric shower yourself, you will need to hire a contractor who is licensed to install showers.

Installing a Digital Shower

You should first turn out the fuses. You can find a suitable location to install your electric shower unit. When you've located the perfect spot, lean the water heater cover against the wall, then trace its outline with a pencil. Don't forget to mark drill holes, pipes, and cables correctly.

Use an electronic detector to check the wall before drilling to be sure you are not going to hit anything. Once the wall has been cleared, you can begin drilling the holes for fixing. Place the pipes and cables in the holes you drilled. If necessary, you can use a reciprocating saw to get everything straight, and then you can use the wall bracket to mark the location for the shower rail holes.

You can turn the cold faucet off and run it till it runs dry. Once the copper piping is connected to the rising main, you can use the compressed tee fixing and an adjustable wrench. You will need to cut a hole in the wall for this step, so that the compressed fixings can fit. Then, in the third arm of the tee, place a stop valve close to it, so that future repairs will be simple.

Attach a flexible hose over the end of the copper pipe and turn off the stop valve, then reconnect the cold-water supply. Afterward, you should flush the new pipe to make sure there are no leaks. Connect the copper pipe to the bottom of the heater unit using an elbow pipe and an adjustable wrench.

Choosing a Shower

Glass enclosures make a shower feel larger by letting in light and allowing the viewer to be more expansive. The interior walls of a shower remain visible from anywhere inside the tub, making a small bath look larger. With a frameless enclosure, you gain a sleek, seamless appearance that is also easier to clean due to fewer spots where soap and grime can collect.

Tub-shower combinations are a good choice when you don't have enough space for a separate shower and tub. Models are available in various shapes and sizes or you can combine your own to create your very own combination with either a tiled or solid surface to surround the tub. Install a glass door over the tub-shower combo, or use a fabric or vinyl shower curtain for extra color and pattern.

Building a Shower Enclosure

To begin with, you must prepare the area for your shower enclosure. Whenever you replace a bathtub or shower, you will have to remove the old materials, including the wall studs and subflooring. You should measure the space available for a new shower enclosure and make sure it is supported properly.

Install 2 x 4 studs if necessary to construct the floors and walls. If you need to install plumbing, make sure you mark the location; if you have to drill holes near the pipes, the existing plumbing will be damaged. You can check the level of the floor by using a level.

The shower-liner should be dry fitted to ensure it fits the desired space. Choose the base or liner you prefer and mark its fit. Installation instructions will be provided with your chosen base.

Replacing a New Bathtub

Make sure to map out the whole bathroom, including any plumbing, including measuring the old bathtub and drawing the floor plan. Your bathtub should be the right size for the space you have. Identify whether the drain is on the left side, right side, or center of the tub area, and mark it accordingly. You can move things around easier on paper than with heavy pieces of bathroom equipment.

Once you remove the old bathtub, you'll need to level the subfloor before placing the new one. Tubs can be removed from small bathrooms by placing them on their side and carrying them vertically out. Taking out the old tub will probably require removing the sink and toilet first. You'll have more space to move.

It's important to match the fit of your fixture and new tub using shims after you've placed the new tub. Before trying to install the tub, dry-fit the drain and drain shoe, as well as most of the tub's plumbing. The majority of the work can be done before placement. Apply caulk all around the perimeter after attaching the drain. Replace the faucet after that.

Water leaks should be checked after filling the bathtub. Please note that mortar, caulking, and plumber's putty must be set completely within 24 hours. Testing for water tightness is best done after all raw materials are cured. Replace any drywall and tiles that need to be replaced, then reinstall the sink and toilet.

CHAPTER 5:

Flooring

I t can be difficult to choose new flooring. Materials come in a wide variety of types, along with a wide variety of options. Additionally, there are a variety of considerations based on the room and the traffic flow.

Flooring 101

Floors can never be completely maintenance-free. It is necessary to vacuum and deep clean the carpet periodically. There is a need to dust, wax, and refinish wood floors from time to time. All ceramic tiles, even those that are hard-wearing, must be grout-sealed and mopped regularly. Consider how your flooring choices feel underfoot and how they sound. Several people have complained about the cold temperature of bare feet on a tiled floor in the bathroom.

Types of Flooring

You need to know what type of installation you are doing if you are doing it yourself. Aesthetics also play a role. Find out where you wish to see seams or grout lines. There are many things to consider when it comes to flooring.

Laminate

Living rooms, kitchens, and playrooms are ideal for laminate flooring. Strong laminate construction resists warping. The deep plastic wear layer protects from scuffs and scratches. It is possible to install them over existing flooring such as ceramic or wood. Installations of this type are easy to do on your own. Unlike real marble, the super-hard surface feels artificial; slippery when wet, and can't be refinished.

Hardwood

Flooring made from hardwood is best suited for living areas, hallways, and kitchens. Floors made from this durable, beautiful, and long-lasting material go with any decor. You can refinish solid wood flooring several times. Hardwood floors do not belong in bathrooms, laundry rooms, or basements due to their susceptibility to moisture. To keep it looking good, it needs constant upkeep.

Vinyl

If you have a kitchen, a bathroom, a basement, and a hobby room, vinyl flooring is the best option. Vinyl flooring is durable and resistant to water. Feels good underfoot, due to its resilient construction. It's not expensive at all. A vinyl plank floor can mimic the look of hardwood or tile. However, producing vinyl flooring is not an eco-friendly process.

Ceramic

Ceramic tile works best in bathrooms, kitchens, and sunrooms. There are countless styles and colors of ceramic tile flooring. It's one of the favorite mediums of designers. Tile flooring made of glazed ceramic is durable, resistant to moisture, and scratch-resistant. Ceramic tile underfoot is hard, making many people dislike it. Grout lines must be kept clean at all times.

Bamboo

The best places to install bamboo flooring are in the main living area, kitchen, and family room. Although bamboo flooring is not wood, it is grass. It provides the same warmth and beauty as wood flooring. The surface is hard, but it's best to look for a quality product to keep it lasting. Since bamboo is grass, it is a renewable resource and has some green properties. A cheaper variety is more likely to be dented and scratched.

Suspended Floors

There are two types of floor construction: suspended or solid. In a suspended timber floor, floorboards are attached to joists, usually on a brick wall. For a suspended floor to remain dry, it must be ventilated from the underside. Suspended floors should focus on improving thermal insulation and preventing draughts. When access is available from below, for example, through a crawl space or basement, insulation can be installed fairly easily.

In most cases, the easiest way to insulate the spaces between the joists is to push quilt-type insulation from below into the interstices. A plastic garden netting is nailed to the frame to support it. To provide additional insulation, tongue-and-groove wood-fiber boards can be attached to the underside of the joists.

Adding insulation from the top is more complex and will require the lifting of floorboards. When it comes to floors that are valuable historically or aesthetically, this can be done carefully but is also likely to cause damage. If you're not doing major work on the house, you should raise only a few boards at a time, otherwise, you'll damage the joists and sleepers below. The spaces between the joists can be filled with quilt insulation by laying garden netting over the joists so it forms troughs. As another option, you can use a breathable membrane and then use cellulose, like recycled newspaper, as an insulation material.

In addition, foil-faced foam and wood fiber battens can be used in place of bubble wrap between joists. In some cases, the insulation can be placed by lifting floorboards.

How to Draught-Proof a Timber Floor

When you install insulation in your home, it will work only if you use the correct type, protect it against moisture, wind washing, and make sure the installation is airtight. Wind washing is when the air is drawn out of the insulation by the vents beneath the floor.

The only thing you need to be aware of when installing insulation is that it does not necessarily block all draughts, so you should seal all gaps; otherwise, you will still feel the cold, and energy will be wasted. There are several draught strips available in most DIY stores that fit between wooden floorboards. Draughts and heat loss can easily be reduced by slotting these into gapped areas.

Solid Wood Floors

DIY projects such as laying solid wood floors are quite feasible, but not every homeowner has the time or inclination to do so. Getting someone to lay the floor for you will involve either hiring a builder or a local carpenter or joiner. Some suppliers can recommend specialists who fit floors.

You need to let the flooring adapt to the room before laying it. For flooring types that should remain in their packaging during acclimatization, contact your supplier for further information. You may also be able to find out how long you have to leave, some require 24 hours' notice, others longer.

The best method of laying a solid wood floor is to fix it, as opposed to floating it. To prevent future problems, solid wood flooring needs to be installed on the subfloor before it moves. Depending on the floor, the bracket can be attached to concrete, floor joists, or timber floor.

When Fixing Wood Floors to Concrete

Level the concrete and make sure it is solid. The best way to install a new wood floor is to screw in a chipboard or plywood sub base, then nail or glue it into place. Gluing down the floor is the best method of fixing it to the concrete. Alternatively, you might want to check out some of the self-adhesive membranes on the market, but be careful, they are incredibly sticky and once the wood is attached to the membrane, it will be near-impossible to remove.

Engineered Timber Flooring

Engineered wood is becoming more and more popular as opposed to solid wood. In comparison with solid timber, it has greater stability and is therefore far less prone to movement. It is constructed with layers of solid wood bonded to layers of softwood, and it comes with tongue-and-groove edges that are clicked together without the need for nails or glue.

Floors can be readily installed as a floating floor over an existing floor or with an underlayment. If there have to be any patches in the near future, it is especially important to have a thick layer of wood on top to prevent future sanding.

Laying a Concrete Floor

It is becoming increasingly popular to install cement flooring in home buildings' bathrooms, kitchens, and outdoor living areas as well. Its versatility is one of its biggest selling points, as homeowners can choose from colored, textured, and stamped cement floors or floors similar to more expensive materials like granite.

Preparing Your Floor

In order to achieve optimal results, surfaces must be prepared properly. Incorrectly installing your new cement surface can cause unevenness or discoloration. Before installing a new cement layer, the old flooring must be removed. Remove all trim and baseboards as well. It is essential that the base is free from dust, old adhesives, paint, grease, cracking, and sealing compounds, as well as any weak cement screed.

You can clean the surface using a mixture of water and hydrochloric acid by pouring acid into the water rather than the other way around, this will avoid a chemical reaction that could splatter. Use a scrub brush to brush the mixture onto the screed base. Make sure there are no cracks, holes, or uneven surfaces on the surface. Make sure the surrounding surfaces are level by placing a spirit level across any cracks.

How to Lay Concrete

Mix in a bucket self-leveling cement, water, and acrylic polymer liquid, as directed by the product manufacturer. An electrical drill can be used to thoroughly mix cement with the concrete mixer drill bit. Then use a steel trowel to apply the mixture in an even layer across the floor.

The cement should be allowed to sit for about 30 minutes before smoothing the surface with a wooden trowel or float. If you wish, you can now apply a color tone. Dry cement pigment should be spread over the newly floated cement so that it does not clump. Spread the powder on the top with a metal trowel or float, and let it sink in. Remove excess powder from the cement by rinsing it with a hosepipe. For those who prefer not to paint their flooring with dry pigment themselves, self-leveling cement comes ready-mixed with different colors.

To further polish the cement, sprinkle drops of water onto the smooth surface if you haven't already added pigment. Depending on the product manufacturer's instruction, dry the cement for a minimum of 10 hours and a maximum of 24 hours. Using a paint roller or lamb's wool applicator, apply an epoxy flooring coating, or a hard wearing protective floor polish as a protective layer on the floor. This will ensure that the floor surface will be durable and resistant to scratches.

To keep yourself safe, one must wear safety goggles and gloves when working with strong chemicals. You should also work in an area with good ventilation. You should also be cautious when using tools.

Staircase Makeover

Adding stairs to a deck, porch, or shed isn't all that difficult from a technical standpoint. The parts can be cut and assembled by anyone with basic carpentry skills. However, building stairs is arguably the most difficult do-it-yourself task.

To ensure safety and climbing comfort, stairs must adhere to strict building codes. Short steps are difficult to climb, and steep steps are dangerous and uncomfortable. A staircase must be laid out carefully, and its calculations must be precise, due to the limited room for error. A typical staircase consists of three components: stringers, treads, and risers.

Stringers, which typically extend from a deck to the soil, are usually made from 2x12s. They carry the weight of people walking up the stairs as well as the weight of the other stair components. A typical staircase has three stringers and is typically 16 inches apart. Always choose a staircase that is wider than it is narrow. Most decks and porches have steps that are at least four feet wide.

Each step is topped by a tread, which is positioned horizontally on top of a riser. Some deck stairs do not have risers, but they are a good idea to install because they help protect the notched stringers from cracking. The stringers that build decks and porches are usually constructed from weather-resistant pressure-treated lumber. Besides treated lumber, the treads and risers can also be made from cedar, redwood, PVC boards, or exotic hardwoods, which can also be used for decking.

Designing Staircases

Staircases, whether indoors or outdoors, must be carefully designed and constructed from the materials of your choice. Modern interior staircases are becoming more open with no walls and artistic handrails. Many staircases combine industrial materials with wood to produce a beautiful, practical, and strong construction. There are many types of treads available, from soft wood to acrylic, on an open tread staircase, without solid risers.

Things to Consider When Constructing Stairs

The stairs you build must be supported by a strong framework unless they are poured concrete. There are a variety of wood stringers available, but most are designed to look like saw blades. A staircase is usually made out of 2-foot by 12-foot pieces of lumber, reinforced with bolts on both the bottom surface and the upper floor level.

Stringers are supported by vertical risers made of wood. There are treads on each horizontal level each of which is securely screwed, forming a stepped box-like structure. For staircases that won't be completely enclosed, straight-edge supports can replace the sawtooth stringer, and for an industrial look, the treads can be bolted to the railings or attached with metal connector slots.

Repairing Indoor Wooden Steps

As the hardwood ages, it is subject to damage such as cracks, splits, gouges, and moisture infiltration. Most problems can be solved by following a few simple techniques.

Dent Repair

Denting is one of the most frustrating problems with wooden steps. You can steam dents up to 1/4 inch and they'll be completely removed. This is a common practice among professionals. Water a few drops into the dent. Use a hot iron to iron a folded cotton cloth on top of the dent. By moving the iron in circular motion over the dent, steam will rise upward. The iron should be moved until no steam comes out. Keep track of your progress. You may repeat the procedure until the dent is gone. Dents are filled by swelling of wood fibers as they absorb water.

Dutchman Method

There is a thin piece of hardwood of the same species as a tread or riser that is called a Dutchman. Cracks or splits with a diameter of 1/8 to 1/4 inch can be spliced with a Dutchman splice. You can use a knife or a bandsaw to shave or cut thin slices of hardwood. Rather like cracks, slices should taper as they go from one end to the other. Then, using a few of them, compare each slice to the crack until you find a piece that is similar to the crack. With 100-grit sandpaper, shape the slice, letting it just be wider than the crack.

You can taper one edge so that it fits into cracks when it's similar in shape. Glue some wood glue liberally into the crack, then pound a Dutchman down into it. There's nothing wrong if the Dutchman breaks and hammers flat. Even the smallest pieces and pieces of glue, mixed together, can fill any void. Let the glue dry, and then use a chisel to remove any debris. The Dutchman can be colored with a stain marker when it is finished.

Using Resin Glue

Resin glue is the best choice for narrow cracks, splits, or cracking that is a series of small cracks closely spaced. Resin glue is also suitable for honeycomb, which consists of small holes in a pattern. You can also have this glue colored to match the kind of wood you have. Incorporate resin glue into the water as instructed by the manufacturer. When it's ready, it will be thick like pancake syrup. Make sure cracks and splits are thoroughly saturated with resin glue using a small brush or putty knife. If any excess glue remains on the tread or riser, wipe it lightly with a damp cloth. The glue will dry to the consistency of glass overnight. There is no way to tell it apart from natural wood grain.

Consider Using Wood Filler

Gouges should be filled with hardwood filler. Combined with real wood fibers, this solid material is sturdy, durable, and made from plastic. It is available in a variety of colors to complement your treads and risers. You can use it if you have scratches or gouges of up to 1/4 inch in depth. Push it into the defect with a putty knife until it is compressed so that the filler actually rises about 1/6 inch above the surface of the wood. After the filler has dried completely, use 100-grit sandpaper followed by 180-grit sandpaper to sand it flush with the surface. The patch can be colored with a marker if you need to do so.

Replacing a Balustrade

Step 1: Remove the Current Balustrades

Your existing balusters should be sawed out. A handsaw can be used to cut the baluster just enough to allow you to pull it out with ease. Removing any nails that are remaining after removing the old balusters may require the use of pliers. Make sure the underside of the handrail is free of damage.

Step 2: Drill New Holes for the Balusters

The underside of the handrail holes should be large enough for the new balusters, so only the base rail holes need to be drilled. You can test your drilling success by inserting a baluster into the hole after it has been drilled. There is no need to worry if the hole is larger than the baluster. It will be covered up by the metal shoes.

Step 3: Sand the Base Rail

Sand at the intersection of the old balusters and the base rail. Any large paint globs can be peeled off with a flathead screwdriver before you sand. Sand the non-painted section until it has a smooth transition to the painted section.

Dust should be removed by wiping the surface or vacuuming.

Step 4: Make Measurements

Make sure the new balusters are the right height. Adding 1 inch to the distance between the handrail and the top of the base rail will do the trick. There is no harm in checking every few balusters to ensure they are all the same size.

Step 5: Paint the Base Rail

Your base rails should be painted where you sanded them down. If necessary, apply more coats. If you're using high-gloss paint, after you paint over all of the sanded spots, use an additional coat to minimize brush strokes. When the paint has dried completely, move on to the next step.

Step 6: Trim the Balustrades

Using a metal cutting blade on the saw, cut the new balusters to the correct size. Double-check the size of the first baluster after it has been cut. Blue tape can help you identify where to cut the balusters to avoid damage from the saw blade.

Step 7: Setup the New Balustrades

After drilling the holes in step 3, insert the new balusters. You will need to slide your shoe over the baluster, add some liquid nails into the handrail hole, and then insert the baluster into the handrail and base rail holes. The shoe can be slipped down to the base rail and tightened so it stays in place. You can prime and paint the balusters after they have dried completely.

Repairing Balusters

Wooden balusters that have split may be repaired by removing them and gluing them. Either the nails or a piece of wood from the underside of the rail will need to be removed, depending on the staircase construction.

A cracked baluster may be repaired by applying wood glue to the crack and using padded clamps to close the crack until the glue sets. If the gap is too large, it might be a good idea to check that you can close it before applying glue. The baluster should be straight and should not be twisted before the glue sets, so if it is, you should correct it. When the glue has set, either attach the baluster with nails or replace the wood fillet.

Handrails

A handrail should at least be installed on one side of stairways less than 1 m wide. If the steps are wide, a handrail should be on both sides. On the first two steps, a handrail is not necessary. The only time a wall-mounted handrail is needed is if your stairs are narrower than one meter, or if they are against only one wall. Home staircases are usually narrower than this; so, in most cases, you won't need a wall-mounted handrail.

How to Fit a Handrail

To determine the height required for a handrail, check your local building codes. Mark and measure the walls at the bottom and top of the stairs. Draw a chalk line connecting the marks. Stud finders can be used to locate and mark wall studs. Make sure the brackets are plumb by marking their locations on a level.

Position the railing along the chalk line with the help of a friend, then attach the bracket. An awl can be used to punch holes in the mounting holes of the brackets. Prepare the wall by drilling pilot holes and mounting brackets. Install the long and short rails and level the shorter piece using the clamps.

For both rails, measure the angles using a combination square. You can create a paper template of the angles required to join two railing lengths, then mark the rail ends. Use a handsaw to cut both pieces on the same day for even cutting. A miter box should be used to cut the rail at a 45-degree angle at the upper and lower ends. Make sure the railing comes to a point where it returns to the wall so items will not catch on it.

Apply glue to both ends of the rail and to the returns. Secure returns with screws and L-brackets. The rail should be secured to brackets with screws. Install the short rail on wall brackets after applying glue to the top end of the rail. During the drying process, tape the joint to prevent it from moving. Make sure a metal plate is installed under the railing to strengthen the joint.

CHAPTER 6:

Storage and Appliances

Wall installations are a different matter from DIY craft projects. It is easy to build these DIY wall shelves without a drill or hammer. You can create storage space in your home by using pegboards or hexagonal shelves.

Pegboard shelves are great for displaying vases, plants, mirrors, frames, etc., and a giant wood wall covering will add a touch of warmth to your space. Hexagon shelves are made out of popsicle sticks and don't need a drill, which makes them an easy DIY project.

Shelving and Storage

Adding open shelving to a room, even if it's just in a corner, will update the entire look. An open shelving system is both a classic and trendy idea. It would be great if you could add something that would take your kitchen from bland to beautiful just by adding open shelving. Open shelving creates an instant focal point in the kitchen.

Show Off Cooking Books and Memorable Pictures

The amount of books and magazines that pile up quickly is something you're probably aware of if you read offline. However, they do not necessarily have to become a source of clutter. Choose books that you love to read and use them for shelf display. To boost the color palette of your room, use your books to create a color story. You should arrange your shelf items so that they differ in height for a larger visual impact. Add an eye-catching piece of art or an elegant vase to your display.

Making a Loft Hatch

In addition to being very useful for gaining access to the roof space, a loft hatch is often small and needs upgrading with a larger one. You will need to measure the hole and make a box that will fit inside of the hole that you just made.

To make the loft liner, cut four pieces of timber to fit in the loft hole. You then join the pieces using butt joints. Miter joints are possible if you have a good saw. The timbers need to be one inch thick. Make a lip on the inside of the box by cutting four pieces of 1-1/2-inch timber on each side and nailing them onto the inside of the box to make a push-up lid.

Using four pieces of architrave, cut each corner off and mitre it before nailing it to the box you just built. All that remains is to screw the loft hatch into position, and then it will be ready! To make a hinged lid, just cut the plywood to the correct size and hinge one edge before fitting a catch to keep it shut.

Working With Electricity

Our lives depend on electricity. We use it every moment of each day. Because of this, we forget that it can be powerful and dangerous. Many DIY errors lead to electric shocks, including cutting through cables, drilling into wiring, and repairing electric appliances while they are switched on.

Averting Safety Hazards

Nearly half of all severe electricity shocks in homes are caused by DIY projects. There's no reason you shouldn't do your electrical work. Most homeowners agree that basic household wiring doesn't have to be difficult. You need to be careful, but it's not complicated.

- One of the most common ways to harm your electrical system is by misuse of kitchen appliances.

- It is not a good idea to mix water and electricity. Among the most dangerous rooms in a house for electrical safety is the bathroom. It is best to wait until it is dry outside before using electrical gardening equipment.

- Flooded homes have a high chance of having their electricity damaged.

- You should be cautious of electrical fires and constantly check the condition of your cables. In case you see burnt wires around your house, it is best to call a professional to replace them.

- Working with insulated tools is always a good idea.

- Other effective precautions include putting rubber mats on the floor. The soles of rubber shoes and gloves are non-conducting. The nonconductivity of rubber prevents you from getting shocked.

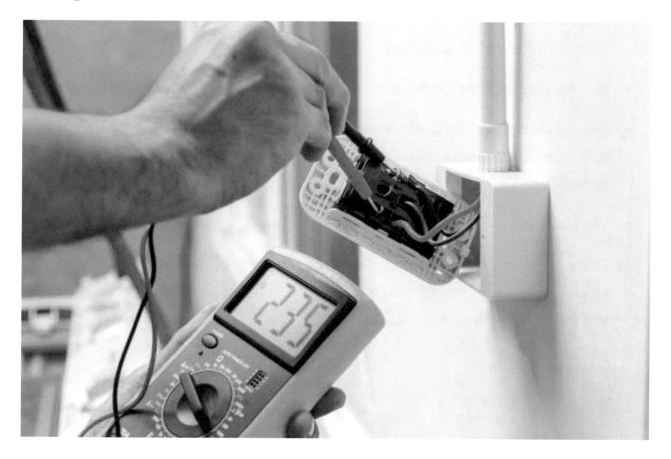

A neon circuit tester is one of the simplest devices on the market. The neon light is inside the small body, and two short wires are attached to each end with metal probes. Voltage testers for neon bulbs only indicate whether the voltage is present—they do not indicate how much voltage is present. The wire probes on this tool are not non-contact, as the screw terminals and outlet slots need to be touched for it to work. The battery-free nature of this device makes it highly reliable.

You will need to touch the test probe to the hot wire, screw terminal, or outlet slot on one side, and the neutral or ground side on the other side. If the tool is getting current, the neon bulb will light up.

You should handle this tool with caution: If you accidentally touch one of the metal probes during a test without knowing that there's voltage present, you can get shocked. The probes of a neon circuit tester must be carefully held by the plastic casing. Even if you also own a non-contact tester, you should own this tester because it is affordable.

Assessing Your Installation

Your wiring may need to be upgraded if your lights are flickering or your switchboard trips often. If this happens, you should check to see whether your home's electrical wiring is up to today's standards. It is not only an inconvenience but also a risk to your safety if your house has bad wiring.

Checking the wiring in your home visually can help you find bad wiring. Wiring that is frayed or ripped may be an indication that there are problems. If you notice flickering or buzzing lights, you may have burnt power outlets.

A certified electrician should be consulted if you see any of these things. Wires that are bad can cause fires if you don't thoroughly inspect them. A qualified electrician can examine the problem.

Fuse Boards

An electrical outage in one or more areas of your home is the most obvious sign of a blown fuse. Fuse switches do not operate like breakers. A fuse typically has a small window to allow you to see what's inside. In the fuse window, you will see either melted metal or scorch marks if the fuse blows. It shows when there has been a melt-through in the metal strip.

A standard fuse panel provides 30 or 60 amps of power, but the required minimum for homes with modern appliances is 150 amps, preferably 200. The presence of a fuse box indicates that your electrical service is quite old and not sufficient for modern appliances. When a new fuse blows, the wiring or appliances connected to it are probably malfunctioning. The problem may be related to other appliances connected to the problematic fuse.

Simple Replacements

House wiring is protected from overheating and fire by circuit breakers. When the cause of the overload is resolved, the breaker can be reset to its closed position. With basic mechanical skills and common tools, circuit breakers can be replaced.

Changing the Breaker

Step 1: Disconnect the circuit. To cut the electrical service, it must be turned off outside the house. The interrupt is located inside a locked meter box, and in most cases, the box belongs to the power company. Please contact the local electric company for assistance.

Step 2: The breaker box cover should be removed. Remove the two screws connecting the black wires to the main breaker. To prevent wires from touching panel components, bend them outward.

Step 3:A flat screwdriver can be used to pry up one side of the breaker. Once the breaker has come free, roll it outward. Breakers should now easily come out of breaker boxes.

Step 4: Push the new breaker in until it snaps into place. The breaker will lie flat in a plane with the others. Turn off the new breaker.

Step 5: To install a circuit breaker, connect the two large, black wires. The screws must be torqued tightly, but not over tightened, in order to prevent them from stripping. Having re-established electrical service, carefully examine the breaker box to see if it is smoking or arcing. Check to see if you have power to the house circuits by turning on the main breaker.

Socket Outlets

You might need to replace your electrical outlets if they are worn, damaged, or faulty. Installing upgraded outlets eliminates that danger and increases your home's energy efficiency. Before you begin working, make sure the power is off at home. A screwdriver is required for the job, either a Phillips head or a flat-head screwdriver.

Electrical cables in the home have three wires:

- Linking green/yellow with the earth terminal (E)

- Blue is Neutral (N)

- The live terminal is on brown (L)

To cut the wires, you'll need a wire-cutter or a flexible tool like a Leatherman. If you are attaching a screw-hole terminal, remove the plastic insulation, which will expose approximately five mm of wire. You can tidy up your wire by tying loose copper strands together.

When using screw-in terminals, make sure to place each wire in its corresponding hole and tighten the screws. Make sure your toolbox is stocked with multiple screwdrivers because you'll need them for this. Each wire should be wound around each pillar, and then tightened with a screw. Connect all the wires to the correct terminals, and make sure all the wires are neatly tucked away with no loose ends. After you've finished, reinstall the plug cover.

Doorbells and Chimes

A new chime can be easily changed whether your old one stopped working or you just want something new. If a remote doorbell malfunctions, it can be fixed by simply replacing the receiver's batteries.

If you need to replace a sound device, follow these steps:

Step 1: The doorbell should be turned off at the service panel. Wires should be taped and labeled for reinstallation.

Step 2: Take the wires off the terminals by loosening the screws.

Step 3: Remove wall-mounted bells or chimes with a screwdriver.

Step 4: Replace the unit by putting the wires behind it. It should be attached to the wall. If you attach wires clockwise, make sure the end is looped around the terminal screw.

Step 5: Ensure that the wires connected to the correct terminals are marked previously.

Step 6: Screw the screws in place, then tighten them. The new unit's cover should be put on.

Step 7: Switch on the power and try the doorbell.

Wiring a Cooker

All electric cookers that consume over 3kW must be hardwired into a dedicated electrical circuit with a separate power switch. If you feel competent enough in DIY, you can install the cooker yourself, but if there is no existing circuit, you may need to have one installed. Circuits for cookers can only be installed by a licensed electrician.

The first thing you should do is determine where the oven is plugged in. You will have to unplug that and turn it off. Four screws should be visible when you open the oven door. You will need to remove all the screws from the oven carcass using your screwdriver. Once the screws have been removed, the oven will need to be carefully removed from its place. Depending on how heavy the oven is, you may need assistance. The plug attached to the oven must be free of worktops and cabinets when removing it. Your old oven's plug will need to be swapped over for your new one.

With the new oven now in place, you can start using it. Be sure to feed the wire from the cooker to the plug. Use your screwdriver to drive your screws into the points on the new oven door, then secure the oven in place. The electric oven can now be switched on once it has been plugged into the wall. The timer on the settings should be set correctly. If you are having trouble setting up your oven, please refer to the manufacturer's instructions.

Wiring Small Fixed Appliances

A leaking refrigerator on your floor is a very dangerous situation. If water is noticed on your floor, you will risk electric shock or falling.

Repairing a Leaky Fridge

It could be a variety of things causing water to leak from your fridge. Perhaps the drain system of the self-defrosting freezer is clogged. Begin by unplugging the refrigerator. Take the drainage pan out of the defrosted water drain. In order to collect melted water, remove the cover panel and locate the drain tube or channel. After removing the drain tube, remove the upper part of it. To remove clogs caused by ice, you can defrost the tube and use a hairdryer. If there is a physical obstruction, use air to force the clog out.

Communication Equipment

You can test your internet speed with many tools to determine if your Wi-Fi is sluggish. Alternatively, you can use some tricks to troubleshoot the problem. If your Wi-Fi isn't performing as expected, there could be a problem with the internet coming into your house. Using an Ethernet cable, connect your computer directly to your modem.

Test your internet speed by running a speed test. A modem that isn't matching the speed of your internet bill may need to be replaced or you may have to contact your ISP. It may be time to pay more for an internet plan if your speed test and internet bill are the same. If the modem seems to be working, try running the tests wirelessly when standing right next to the router. It is possible that your Wi-Fi coverage is to blame if you aren't getting the same speeds in other parts of your house as your router. Even standing right next to the router, your internet might still be slow if some of your gear is outdated.

Installing Wifi Routers

The most common way to install a WiFi device so that you can use it with a laptop is to connect the router using the same computer as your broadband modem; this way, the automated configuration software can access the information it needs without the need for intermediaries.

This is the typical setup:

Disconnect your broadband modem from the power source. If the device has no on/off switch, disconnect its power supply. Power up the wireless router by plugging in the power adapter. An AC outlet should be connected to the adapter. If the LED is lit, the power is on.

Connect the broadband modem to an Ethernet cable. You should now be able to use your modem. You can connect the Ethernet cable to the WAN (wide area network) port on the wireless router's back panel. The other Ethernet cable should be connected between LAN Port 1 (on the wireless router's back panel) and any available Ethernet port on the laptop.

The laptop should be shut down. Start the WiFi-connected laptop again. Launch your internet browser. You need to type the URL of the router's setup screen into the address bar of your browser. The website address for most D-Link routers is http://192.168.0.1. The manufacturer of your device may require you to enter a user name like admin as well as a password. You can find more details in the instructions.

Telephone Extensions

Always isolate the mains supply before repairing.

1. You need to remove the existing switch or socket.

2. The interior of the wall box should be cleaned of any plaster dust and debris.

3. Whenever possible, use a cable that has the correct rating.

4. Before wiring a socket or a switch, check the location of the terminal connections because the layout may differ.

5. When plugs and switches come with a clear plastic gasket, position it between your wall and the accessory. Before connecting the wires to the accessory, this gasket must be placed over them.

6. Install the new socket or switch according to the wiring diagram shown in the fitting instructions. In order to use multicolored cables, ensure that no stray strands are left outside the terminals after they have been tightened. The cable may need to be trimmed and stripped if necessary.

Lighting

You can use lighting to see clearly and also to add aesthetic appeal to your house. Lighting allows you to create an impression in your home by drawing attention to certain details. The right lighting can make any scene more dramatic. The addition of a wall or other object beneath or behind a light will enhance its presence and provide a glamorous halo effect.

It is important to understand the difference between fluorescent lighting and incandescent light. Almost all homes in America have incandescent lights. Offices often use fluorescent bulbs, which are more efficient and last longer.

The Installation of Cable Lighting

When performing electrical work, be sure to turn off the power at the circuit breaker. You can use the following steps to install cable lighting.

1. Using a screwdriver, disconnect the electrical connections and remove any hardware supporting the fixture.

2. Use the ceiling bracket to connect the cable light transformer to the existing electrical box.

3. To connect the ground wire to the ceiling bracket, connect it to the electrical box.

4. Using wire nuts, splice any extension wires into the existing conductors.

5. You will need to feed the wire extension through the center threaded rod of the ceiling bracket and through the transformer center hole.

6. To secure the transformer to the rod, use the supplied nut.

7. Connect the extensions with wire nuts.

8. Connect the transformer canopy to the transformer using the screws provided.

9. Identify the standoff locations by measuring and marking them. Pilot holes can be drilled to ensure there are no structures above. For those without a toggle bolt, make sure the hole is large enough.

10. Connect each standoff with the cable.

11. Each low voltage wire should be tightened with a thumbscrew to add light heads in the desired location.

12. Connect the low voltage cable to the transformer wires.

13. Put the power back on by resetting the circuit breaker.

How to Fix Your Flickering Lights

It is common for light bulb sockets to corrode over time, especially in outdoor fixtures. The lightbulb may flicker if it becomes damaged over time or if it wears out. Check the state of the socket with the switch turned off. A replacement will be needed if the cause of the flickering light isn't the worn-out fixture. There are some LED bulbs that simply aren't compatible with old switches, particularly dimmers. Make sure the dimmer switch you are currently using is LED compatible. In that case, substitute it for one that is.

Installing Dimmers

Dimmer switches are not different from standard switches in terms of how they are replaced. You must use special dimmers for low-voltage lighting if you want to use dimmer switches on fluorescent fixtures.

Ensure the circuit or fuse panel is off by turning off the switch. Once the switch plate is removed, use a voltage tester to confirm that the circuit is not active. You will need to remove the switch whilst it is still connected to the electrical box. Taking apart the old switch will allow you to install the new one. Instead of screw terminals, dimmer switches are typically connected to the house wiring with short lengths of wire coming from their bodies. The black wires from the dimmer switch must be attached to the colored wires that were attached to the terminals on the old switch using the connectors that came with it.

Screw on the wire nut after you have twisted the wires together. Install the new switch in the electrical box by pushing it back into the box and by screwing it up. Dimmer switches have a larger body than their replacements. Make sure you don't push it. To make space for it, you may have to reposition or reorganize wires.

Heating in Your Home

There are several types of fuel used to power heating systems. Electricity, natural gas, biofuel (such as wood), propane, and fuel oil are among them. Many homes have more than one heating system. The most common type of heating system in American homes is the gas furnace, which is estimated to be in about 60 percent of houses. Modern furnaces are capable of delivering extremely high levels of efficiency while older models do not.

Despite their reliability, forced-air furnaces can sometimes malfunction. If you are having problems with your thermostat, make sure it is set to "heat."

It is often confusing and difficult to use programmable thermostats. Before you assume your furnace is the problem, take a look at your thermostat. The switch may also be accidentally shifted when it is being cleaned. Be sure that everything is in order with your thermostat before you make any phone calls.

Make sure the thermostat is set at a temperature that will start the furnace. Let the fan and heat kick in after the temperature is set. You should set the thermostat to 90 degrees if the heater does not come on, so it doesn't turn on and off while you are trying to fix it. If your thermostat isn't working, see if there is a problem with the wiring in your furnace. To repair a wire break, tape it and splice it back together. It is possible that the battery needs to be replaced.

System Repairs and Maintenance

Maintaining a furnace is usually quite straightforward.

1. Ensure the exhaust vents are clean. A blockage in the intake or exhaust of your furnace might be caused by leaves or debris falling from the roof. Remove the screen mesh from the pipes and replace it with a 1/2-inch hardware cloth. In the event that one of your pipes is clogged with ice, it may be a more serious problem. Clean out the ice and contact a professional to assess the problem.

2. Replace the air filters and inspect them. Each month, you should inspect your furnace's air filter and replace it if it appears dirty. When the furnace is too dusty and dirty inside, it can no longer function, or it may not work at all. You should change your filter at least three times a year.

Room Heaters

Most wall heaters can be installed and replaced without major problems. It's usually very simple to install. Just make sure that it is attached to a stud in the wall, not just the sheetrock. A repair can easily be made by taking something down and repairing it.

A great advantage of wall heaters is the fact that the heat usually lasts for hours after turning them off. Inspect your home's insulation and windows for leaks. A wall-mounted heater is not only convenient and cost-effective but also space-saving. Since they attach directly to the wall, they free up more floor space.

Maintaining Your Boiler

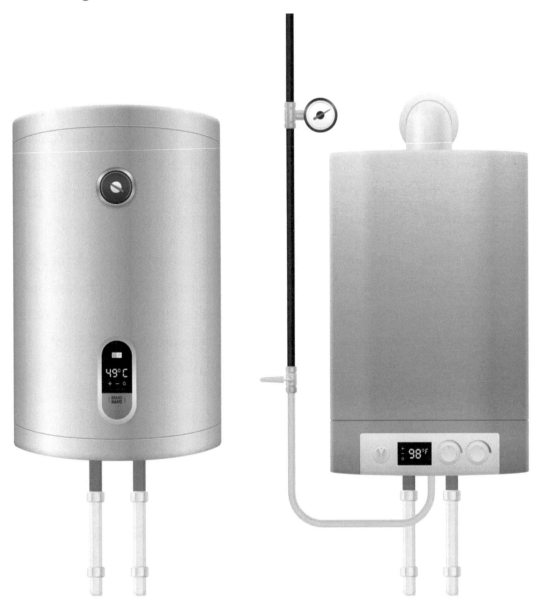

It's common for people to neglect their home's machinery and tools until they break. Since their home is always warm, most homeowners won't worry about their boiler heating system functioning optimally. The safety valve should be checked monthly by lifting the lever, and the hydraulic pressure should be checked annually. Should something go wrong, it's important to have a safety valve handy. You need to ensure that it is working because it can prevent an explosion if the boiler pressure builds up too much.

You must set the valve to open at a pressure below the maximum working pressure set by your manufacturer. The boiler should not be run too close to its valve setting. If it's too close, it leaks, and internal corrosion sets in, preventing the valve from working correctly. By checking the float chamber, you can ensure that the tubing is clear and functioning without restrictions. In the case of damage to the low water fuel cutoff, you may need to have it repaired. As soon as the drain valve is closed, the water level should quickly return to its usual level. If your water is returning slowly, you have a blocked pipe.

When your piping system is installed properly, you will notice a lot of "cross tee" pieces, which make it easier to remove and clean by isolating the cause of buildup and pulling it out as easily as possible. When you are using the boiler, make sure to turn it off, remove cross tees you can access, and clean them out so water flows smoothly. It is not advisable to perform this task on your own if you don't have the right tools.

Home Security

With these new home security systems, you can monitor package deliveries, ensure your kids arrive home safely, and even watch over your house while you're away. When you are away, you can still monitor your home with relatively low-cost methods if you do not want to install a complete smart security system. When it comes to using a camera security system, make sure not to hide your camera. A burglar will often avoid homes where security cameras might be present because they are afraid of being seen.

Guarding Against Intruders

You can secure your home in an inexpensive manner. Using a motion sensor bulb or screwing an adapter between a regular bulb and socket can make regular lights into motion sensors. When placed outdoors, they'll cast a spotlight on anyone scoping out your property, and the sheer visibility alone may be enough to keep them from committing a crime.

Securing Doors and Windows

The door locks should be changed if you move into a house where someone else once lived. You'll be able to ensure your locks are the best on the market while eliminating strangers from having access to your home.

Burglars often enter through doors and windows. Sadly, manufacturer window latches aren't always effective. If you dislike the look of your window latches, consider installing locksets or key-operated levers instead. There's more you can do:

- Glass can be reinforced with window security film.

- Sensors that detect glass breakage should be installed on windows.

- A window bar can be added.

- If you have windows on the first floor, plant prickly bushes.

Protecting Against Fire

You can do a lot to keep fires from starting in your home if you're concerned about losing it to fire. Though accidents may happen, there are ways to prevent them from escalating. You should always install fire and smoke detectors before going into any danger. The smoke and heat sensors in that device on your wall sound an alarm when they sense smoke and heat. By spotting a problem early, you'll avoid an emergency situation.

Change the Batteries as Needed

It is easy to tell when smoke alarm batteries are low. It isn't just for fun when they chirp every few minutes. It's a low battery alert, and you shouldn't ignore it. As a result, your home is at higher risk if a fire breaks out and the smoke detectors batteries run out.

Other Tips to Protect Your House From Fire

Fireplaces are fire hazards in living rooms or dens. Be sure to clean the fireplace and stove and keep them free of fire hazards. Christmas trees near a fire sound cozy, but they can be seriously dangerous if they are not properly protected. The glass windows and metal screen of your fireplace should be open when you use it. In this way, embers cannot jump from the fireplace to your floors, as air enters the fireplace. Make sure you move any logs inside using fire-safe equipment, like iron pokers. Avoid using your hands.

It might seem odd that the laundry room could be a fire hazard, but dryer lint is flammable. In your home, the laundry room is one of the most common places for a fire to start. Overheating is a real possibility with these powerful appliances, especially if their vents aren't regularly cleaned.

CHAPTER 7:

Outdoor Fun

Beautiful landscaping is used everywhere, from quiet residential areas to busy urban areas. Making sure your home looks good from the outside is crucial to its curb appeal, and ensuring that it looks good will boost your property value. There can be no denying that the landscaping of a house affects its asking price.

Gardens

Getting started with a garden may seem intimidating. Whether your yard is big and sprawling, or teeny-tiny, you can find great garden ideas and free garden plans. Firstly, inspect the area where you wish to plant: Does it get full sun, which means it gets six or more hours of direct sunlight per day? Maybe it is only exposed to half the sun, or it is in full shade. For a couple of days, keep an eye on that space to see what's going on at what time. Be aware of seasonal changes, too. A shaded area in the summer may be in full sun in the spring. A plant's ability to thrive in a particular climate will be dictated by that.

Being patient is also critical since gardens do not arise overnight. Plants that you love evolve over time as you learn more about them. Whatever your gardening experience level is, you'll encounter some unexpected twists and turns. Your garden and plants are always something new to learn. Learn how you can create a beautiful backyard by exploring great garden plants and backyard design ideas.

Planning a Garden

The planning of your garden should begin immediately. In this way, you can buy the appropriate seeds, fertilizers, and any other materials you need. You can save seeds from previous years' gardens, or you can dry out your seeds as the year goes on. Take advantage of whatever you have at home. Make a hose watering system using old hoses and cut sticks for stakes. It is best to minimize your garden spending as much as possible before it becomes too expensive.

You should first map the area or areas on your property that you will be gardening. Be sure to observe the daily hours of sunlight for each place, the slopes of the land, and the type of soil. Take exact measurements of the area. With this information, each area can be properly planted with the right kind of plants, depending on the plant's specific needs. Double-check to ensure your plants will grow in the right location and what type you're using. It is not recommended to plant onions and garlic close to beans or peas. It is not a good idea to put short plants between taller ones, since they will block some of the sunlight.

There is a good chance that you do not have a big enough backyard to garden if you live in an urban area. It won't stop you from growing your own micro garden. Gardening within a small space can be done in a number of ways. Put potted plants in your balcony, create window baskets or vertical gardens, or create plant pockets for your exterior walls. Create a luscious urban garden by maximizing every inch of space.

Fencing Your Garden

You can enhance the curb appeal of your home with a fence and add privacy. Your fencing plans should be communicated to your neighbors openly and honestly. If two or more neighbors wish to build a party fence, this should be done in writing and only after some professional determination of the property lines has been made.

Choosing Fences

Be sure that you know how a wooden fence should face when you are constructing one. It is recommended that the neighbor sees the finished, smooth side of the fence. It should be the inside side that has the rails and posts visible. Fences are typically built in this manner. This will not only improve the look of your property but will also impress your neighbors.

White picket fences are classic, yet before you purchase wood posts and whitewash, consider how much work you will put into it. In the long run, wood fences can rot, warp, and require repairs. If you want a wood look without the upkeep, consider using low-maintenance materials. There are other options as well, including aluminum, steel, wrought iron, and bamboo.

Chain-Link Fencing

Whenever this fencing is installed properly, it doesn't need much maintenance. You won't need to worry about it rusting or collecting dirt thanks to its vinyl coating. It may only be necessary to trim the plants that grow along with the links. It is much easier to install chain link fencing than most other types of fencing. This could be an advantage if you're on a tight deadline or you just want the property enclosed quickly.

Growing Hedges

You may want to consider a hedge for your fence. A properly maintained hedge lasts longer than a wooden fence, produces more berries and blooms for wildlife and pollinators, and is more attractive than most walls. Before shopping for supplies, you should decide what type of barrier you need.

If you are considering a fence for safety or privacy, make sure it is 6 feet high at the very least. To ensure compliance with the city or municipal height rules, you should make your plans by those guidelines. The taller the fence, the harder it is to manage. Trimming, shearing, or even spraying them can be challenging. A shorter fence will add more aesthetic value to your property even if it requires less work to maintain.

Erecting a Fence Post

A simple modification of your existing fence posts can add a great deal of value to the fence. You can change the look of a fence by adding something to the posts. Add some character to your fence by hanging planters on your posts.

Most posts are made from wood. You could use cedar, pine, oak, or cottonwood. There are a few tips for installing a fence post:

- Fence posts must be buried at least two feet in the ground.

- In general, about two-thirds of a post is above ground and about one-third below it.

- You should use a post-hole digger to dig holes that are about three times as wide as the posts.

- You can paint your garden wood fence any color, but most are painted red.

- The bottom of the hole should be filled with coarse gravel to allow water to drain easily and prevent the post from rotting.

- Around the hole, fill in a dry cement mix after setting the post.

- Before the cement dries, check vertical alignment with a level.

- Posts should be straight and uniform on both sides.

- The posts can be left for a day or two.

- The horizontal stringers should be attached and leveled.

- After the stringers have been installed, attach the fence material to them.

- Building a wooden fence will require a different method depending on the kind of wood you are using.

Design Ideas For the Main Gate

Gates are generally used to protect gardens, but they serve many other purposes. A well-designed backyard gate should be warm and welcoming, like the entrance to your home. You can add different colored flowers around your gate, like a row of lavender flowers to add a pop of purple.

Installing a Fence Gate on a Brick Wall

Step 1: Position the gate against the brick wall so that it's closed. You may want to ask a friend or family member to hold the gate while you level it with a bubble level. Make sure the gate is plumb before opening it. With a felt-tip marker, mark the hinge mounting holes onto the wall.

Step 2: You can put the gate aside. Use the marker spots to locate holes in the brick. For brick and concrete walls, use masonry wall anchors. Make sure the hole is deep enough to accommodate the entire anchor.

Step 3: Align the holes with the hinges and place them against the wall. You can ask your friend to assist you with this step.

Step 4: Insert the screws into the anchors and tighten them with the screwdriver.

Building Walls

Retaining walls are typically constructed of rock, concrete blocks, or other materials to keep the soil behind them in place. Retaining walls are built for practical reasons, but when they are integrated with your property's landscaping, they can enhance its aesthetics. You can build them using high-quality materials for a relatively low price and they can greatly enhance the value of your property.

Having a retaining wall that is properly constructed can hold up to heavy loads. Installation is quick and it works for a long period without much ongoing maintenance. You can also create beautiful vertical gardens.

Choosing Bricks or Concrete Block

Bricks that are left over after a construction project can be used in the garden. You can have straight paths, or you can have paths that meander through your garden. Bricks in various styles and colors can create a contemporary or classical path, and the combination of two brick colors can create a visually stunning effect.

If you aren't a fan of bricks in your garden, you can use stones. Your property already has some stones and boulders, so group them together into beds with river rocks and add some plants around them. Flowers and rocks contrast beautifully.

You may be surprised at how many different things you can make out of concrete, especially if you are a novice gardener. Concrete is an extremely versatile material. Be sure to wear gloves and a mask whenever you're handling concrete, and avoid adding too much water at the beginning. Concrete will be smooth and functional for your projects if you add water slowly and mix it thoroughly.

Draped Concrete Plant Pots

Rather than throwing away old tea towels, you could turn them into beautiful draped flowerpots. This project is quite simple and a fun project that doesn't need much planning. You simply need to mix your concrete and soak your towel in it. It can be dried by draping it over an old bucket. Pour concrete into the hollowed-out concrete block if you like, or turn the plant pots upside down to have a new flowerpot.

How to Lay a Brick Wall

You will need the following tools to lay brick in your garden: a pencil, brush, mask, a pair of gloves, a hammer, two mason blocks, a spade trowel, and a brick chisel.

Using a mason's line will help you line up bricks perfectly straight. A mason line is attached to two blocks of masonry with slots. Attach the blocks with the line pulled tight to the ends of the brick row. It is recommended that the top of each brick just touches the top of the line. Brick laying is guided by story poles, which are wood strips. Make pencil marks on the pole to mark the height of each course of bricks and the mortar joints.

Put on gloves and wear a mask whenever working with mortar. Each brick layer should receive a generous amount of mortar from a spade trowel. Mark a line through the middle of the pile of mortar so it can spread. Butter the bricks with mortar, covering its sides with the same mortar that will be used to attach them to each other. Make sure each brick is in its proper position by hitting it with the handle of a trowel and releasing any air bubbles in the mortar. Make sure all excess mortar that extends beyond the joint is scraped off with the trowel's sharp end. Use a brush to remove any other debris. Use a spade trowel to carve small lines between bricks and mortar at a 30-degree angle. These lines will serve as a shield for the wall against precipitation.

The ends of a wall require smaller bricks. Placing the brick in a bed of sand or dirt makes it less likely to crack. Use a brick chisel to cut across the cut line. Then tap the chisel at the end, making lines on each side of the brick where it must be cut. As soon as the lines are scored, place the chisel on one of them, slightly angled toward the side of the brick that is to be used on the wall. By striking the handle with a hammer with your other hand, you will make your chisel's blade more durable. When the brick is struck, it should split cleanly in two. You should have a perfectly solid mortar in 48 hours.

Paths, Drives, and Patios

An outdoor living area is much easier to construct than one indoors. You don't have to struggle with walls, ceilings, doors, or windows in the backyard. A floor is really all you need. One of the first steps in designing a patio is to choose what type of underfoot surface to use, usually brick, concrete, stone, or gravel. You need to carefully consider the material you select for your patio before choosing the style, the cost, and how to maintain it.

Concrete Paving

Concrete pavers have many easy-to-cast colors, sizing, and shapes, and are an attractive, cost-saving option. It is possible to apply different textures and finishes to concrete, including salt, etchings, and hand carving. Even simple objects, such as rakes and brooms, can be used to create attractive textured surfaces.

Where to Lay a Concrete Slab

Generally, ready-mix crack-resistant concrete mix is the best material to use for constructing concrete slabs. The ingredients in ready-mix concrete are gravel, sand, cement, and other additives.

You can use concrete in your home's yard in other ways than just as a driveway or sidewalk. Whether you need to build a deck or support something heavy, concrete may be the answer.

Hot tubs can become heavy when they're filled with people and water. As you soak in that hot tub, you could eventually feel a bit lopsided as the hot tub sinks and settles. It's a good idea to place a concrete slab beneath your hot tub to protect it from sinking.

When to Pour a Concrete Slab

Concrete slabs should be poured only in dry, warm conditions. For ready-mix concrete, a high temperature of 70 degrees Fahrenheit must be maintained for at least five days after pouring. During colder temperatures, the slab can be poured, but the curing time is longer.

Timber Decking

You'll find decking a lot easier to lay than most materials. Having a deck can extend the length of your home, giving you more outdoor entertaining space. Having a level surface simplifies the process of laying decks. Whether you want to spend the summer basking in the sunshine or have a cool getaway, you must consider the sun's position throughout the day as you can either chase it or run from it. There's no need to cut down trees or plants, but you can work around them. You want to make sure your decking is not damaged by roots, so you should do your research first. Rather than laying your decking where you think it will look best, try arranging your furniture in a way that mimics what it will appear like if it were decked.

Outdoor Paving Ideas

You can think of paver construction as putting together puzzle pieces. A patio made from bricks in the sand is easy to build and doesn't require a lot of experience. You can increase the value of your home while expanding the living area of your home, providing family and friends with entertainment areas, and expanding your living space. Bricks in the sand can also be used to create a flat, convenient pathway on rainy days.

Flagstone

Pave your walkways with flagstone pavement and neatly trimmed grass for a particularly stunning look. Even though constant care will be necessary to keep your lawn healthy and short, the flagstone will benefit from defining the shape and beauty of the grassy areas.

Garden Steps

Your outdoor landscaping can be enhanced greatly by adding DIY steps and stairs, whether they are flat or sit on a slope. Steps in a garden provide access to different levels and also function as a walkway. You can DIY garden stairs based on your likes and according to the theme of the garden, since garden stairs are less formal than indoor stairs. Stairs are most commonly built with stone as the material. Stone steps and stairs look like they are naturally formed. The steps may also be constructed with wooden planks, timber, bricks, or concrete.

Water Gardens

A garden with water features, such as a waterfall or pond, provides a calming environment. You will feel as if you're walking into your own private backyard oasis when you view a well-designed water garden.

Constructing Ponds

Miniature garden ponds should be placed where they can receive four to six hours of direct sunlight. By doing this, you will be able to keep the pond healthy and clean. You should build your ponds at least two feet deep when building small ones. Based on the space in your garden, it may be wide or narrow. A miniature pond should have at least three feet in width.

You should dig down one foot in the pond if you are planning to keep water plants there. Next, start digging down one foot from the pond's edge. Plastic sheeting that is thick, flexible, and waterproof can line small backyard ponds. Pond liners can be found at hardware stores and farm supply stores. Fill the hole with the liner and push it up against the whole's sides.

The pond should be filled with water, and you should turn on the filter or fountain if necessary. Add fish and plants after the pond has sat for one week. Chlorine in the water can be evaporated this way. The plants in your pond will help keep it cleaner and prettier. Ponds with fish make excellent backyard additions. It will not take long for the fish to grow to fit the size of the pond.

Creative Ideas for Ponds

An inexpensive backyard pond form doesn't have to cost a fortune. You can easily convert an old plastic container into your garden pond, saving you money. It's easy to create a lovely, budget-friendly garden pond with a fountain, some rocks, and something to go around the edges. Adding some lighting can also create a zen atmosphere.

A vintage tank is a wonderful idea to use for a pond. It's so easy to set up that it won't take you more than a few hours. This can be done by burying the tank or by leveling it first and then filling it with water. You can easily build a garden pond from rocks and plants for just a fraction of the cost of one that was designed professionally.

CHAPTER 8:

Other D.I.Y. Improvement Techniques

One of the biggest benefits of building a new home or taking on a renovation project is that you can personalize every detail to reflect the needs and preferences of your family. When you begin to plan your dream home, you have plenty of new features to take into consideration.

Insulation

Even though wall insulation is the best remedy to maximize your home's heat source, there are a number of other DIY insulation that won't cost you a lot of money. Using common household items, you can make a "door snake" to sit at the bottom of your door and block cold air. You can make door snakes out of items as simple as old socks and pillow stuffing.

Blackout curtains can reduce the heat generated in your home. As an alternative to buying all-new curtains, you can line your existing curtains with cheap materials, such as fleece or a PVC shower curtain. During the day, keep your curtains open to allow the sun to shine through and heat up your home, and draw them at dusk to keep the warmth inside.

Insulating Roofs

A lot of heat escapes from most homes into the attic, where it doesn't do you any good. You can lower costs by insulating your attic space with foam, but it can also be done with a simple reflective foil material. The simplest and cheapest way to insulate an attic with even joist spacing is to install rolls of blanket roof insulation between the joists if it is dry. You can use mineral wool, recycled materials, or glass fibre.

Insulating Walls

Most homes built before the year 1990 had two brick walls built with a gap between them. The original cavity wall structure was not insulated. It's easy to find out if you have wall insulation in your house. Look around the walls for signs such as circular holes or ask an installer to check it out.

There is sometimes a government grant available for filling cavity walls. Installers usually drain the cavity and fill it with the filler before they seal up the holes they drilled. As the beads are made of polystyrene, they do not absorb water, so you don't have to worry about dampness. Heat is retained within your home and is not lost to the outside. Therefore, your house will be warm, but the aesthetics and hassles will remain the same.

Soundproofing

The sound is not only reflected by walls but also by hard floors. In rooms with hard surfaces, like wood, tile, and laminate, the simplest way to absorb noise is by putting down an area rug. Thick rugs have an advantage over thin ones. To keep the sound from spreading under the rug, you should purchase an extra thick pad. Consider adding sound-absorbing panels to the walls, and if needed, the ceiling, if you don't mind adding an industrial look to the room. Acoustic panels are made of superior materials that reduce noise, including cork, soft foam rubber, and textiles made of polyester fiber.

Ventilation

When a house is not properly vented, the interior will get wet quickly. First, the water will accumulate on the windows, walls, and ceilings, before trickling into everything else. Mold and mildew will grow inside the house if this water is left unchecked. Often, condensation forms on windows, but it can also be reduced by opening the window. If you don't have vents in your home, opening the windows every morning will do your room some good. If you notice mold building up on your walls and inside cupboards, you can use this simple inexpensive trick. Make sure the bathroom fan is running if you are in the bathroom. Turn the fan on in the kitchen if you are cooking. You will cut down on how much moisture you create every day if you do this.

When it comes to choosing a HVAC system, a system that is too big actually ends up generating excess moisture. On hot and humid summer days, swamp coolers will also create moisture, but an AC system with the correct size will draw moisture out of the air.

Infestation

Pest infestations leave behind some signs of their presence. Observe smeared droppings on fabrics and paper, or grime buildup on walls. If you notice any strange odors in your attic, basement, or crawlspace, then you should investigate. The best home for a bug is a place with food and water. It's likely that they will move in if they find these in your house. A common infestation inside a home is caused by insects such as cockroaches, flies, silverfish, and spiders.

Eradicating Pests

Bugs can be found anywhere in your home, but most of them live in your kitchen. An ant infestation should be handled as quickly as possible. The market is full of ant sprays, but many have chemicals that can harm you and your pets. Try using kitchen cupboard items as an ant repellent.

Make a spray bottle out of half white vinegar and half water. Apply this to any ants that you come across. After that, wipe it down with a damp cloth. Vinegar will interfere with the ants' sense of smell, which will prevent them from returning. To disrupt ants' sense of smell, and to prevent your home from smelling like vinegar, sprinkle cayenne pepper or brewed coffee grounds near the ant nest. They prevent the ants from sensing both your food and other ants in the house. They also have a powdery texture that keeps ants away.

There are many types of unwanted house bugs, but cockroaches are the most common. Cockroaches dislike catnip because of its strong smelling oil. You can also use cotton balls with nepetalactone essential oil on them as a way to fill small satchels. Put these bags in places where you've seen the roaches.

You can kill fleas by dehydrating the fleas with salt if you have a flea problem. Salt your carpets with finely ground salt. Wait a day before vacuuming. Alternatively, you can spray rosemary and lemon juice onto the floor. Boil four cups of water and move it to a bowl. Slice six lemons thinly, chop rosemary leaves and add four to five drops of Geranium essential oil. Leave overnight under a cover. After straining the water, fill a spray bottle with it. You can use this natural solution to repel fleas all around your home.

You may also want to get rid of bed bugs by using baking soda. Baking soda will absorb the moisture in bed bugs, causing them to die. Make sure the area is well-sprinkled with baking soda. Let sit for 30 minutes, then vacuum. This process should be repeated every couple of days to ensure all bugs have been removed.

Fungal Attack

Black mold can be removed with tea tree oil, which is often used for dusting off spiders. Mold spores cannot be re-grown when using this fungicide. It works as a cleaner, and it has the strength to prevent them.

The quantity of tea tree oil to water should be diluted to a ratio of 1 teaspoon per cup of water. Fill up a spray bottle with a shaken mixture and pour it on the area with mold.

It is safe and natural to prevent black mold growth with hydrogen peroxide. The product contains antiviral, antibacterial, and antifungal properties and is safe to use. Mold can grow on clothing, fine fabrics, and porous materials. Add one part hydrogen peroxide and two parts water to a spray bottle. This solution can also be applied directly to the mold growth by soaking a towel in it. After 10 minutes, rinse the area with water. Any mold that remains should be wiped away with a towel.

Damp and Condensation

Condensation is the root cause of dampness. When temperatures drop, condensation forms on windows, creating moisture that eventually leads to mold growth. Wet rooms have a musty smell. Once a door is open, you won't have any trouble spotting it. You may get damp if you notice dark spots on the wall. As a result of moisture in the wall, damp can also manifest as discolored plaster. The wallpaper on your walls is likely to curl away from them due to internal moisture, which is a sign of dampness.

Wet Rot and Dry Rot

Water rot occurs when the wood is exposed to excess moisture for too long. Wood that has been wet for a long time will soften as a result of this type of decay. Typical wet conditions include roof defects, plumbing leaks, or leaking or blocked gutters. Wet rot is often characterized by:

- An unpleasant odor of dampness

- Wood with a spongy feel

- Dry cracks may crumble when touched

- Timber that is darker than its surroundings

Dry Rot

Among all forms of fungal decay, dry rot is the most dangerous. In buildings, it attacks the wood, eating away the parts of it that give the wood its strength. Dry rot in homes, then, is often the result of leaking gutters & downpipes, penetrating damp, and inadequate ventilation. You can experience dry rot symptoms, such as:

- Grey-white skin tinged with lilac and yellow patches.

- White mycelium covering the wood in a fine & fluffy pattern. Among the mycelium, brittle strands may appear.

- Fruiting body similar to a mushroom—soft and fleshy, often orangey in color, with pores, and rust colored in the center.

If your timbers are severely damaged, you may have to replace them. A fungicide will usually stop most cases of wet rot. Wet rot is treated by applying fungicides during the drying out process. In order to treat and get rid of dry rot in masonry, the best product is water dissolved Boron powder. The boron solution can be applied either by brushing or spraying it on the affected masonry, depending on the size of the area and your preference. Proper ventilation and insulation are critical to preventing rot in your attic.

Dealing With Damp

It is possible to prevent cracks, subsidence, dry rot, and environmental damage by installing damp proofing. This will ensure less expensive repairs later on and will make your home more comfortable and safe. There are also other simple solutions to help you deal with dampness in your home:

1. Fix gutters and make sure water does not run down exterior walls. Ensure that your home's sills are in good working order to prevent water from flowing down your walls.

2. Turn on the heating and let the house dry out. Preventing condensation is easier if you keep the temperature stable. Having a leak can cause dampness to stay around for six months, so keep this in mind.

3. Keep your wall surfaces free of vegetation. Wisteria and ivy growing on your home's exterior may look attractive, but can cause dampness and root damage, as well as increase the chances of rot.

Interior Plasterwork

Getting a plastered wall perfect requires practice, but this is something that can be learned. That does not mean it can't be done by someone with no previous experience. It will also help make the process of wet wall plastering much faster and more efficient if you use new plasterboard instead of plastering old walls.

Mixing Plaster

You will need half a bucket of clean water to mix with half a bag of finishing plaster. Mix the contents using your paddle and drill. Make sure that you mix the plaster thoroughly and reach all the lumpy or dry areas. As you are mixing, add more plaster a little at a time. You want to reach a smooth, rich, and creamy consistency as you get closer to a finished mixture. You can add more plaster, one handful at a time if it is still too wet. Once you make your mix, you have approximately 40 minutes to use it. You will need to make a new batch if the original gets too dry.

Installing Plasterboard

If you install new plasterboard instead of plastering over an old wall, you will be saving yourself a great deal of time and minimizing the need for traditional wet wall plastering. To start with, you'll need to cut the plasterboard to size. If you're attaching it to a stud wall, cut it to the middle of the noggin.

Take the sheets and measure them 12mm less than the ceiling-to-floor height. On the ivory side of the plasterboard, mark the cutting line, then cut along it using a straightedge and craft knife. Then turn the plasterboard over and fold one end along, then snap the board to secure it. The paper backing can be cut through using a craft knife.

Attaching the plasterboard to the frame is much easier with someone helping. With your foot, wedge a bolster chisel at the foot of the board, slide a piece of wood underneath and press down hard so the board is forced hard up against the ceiling. Make sure the ivory side of the plasterboard faces out.

In order to install the board, use 32mm plasterboard screws approximately 150mm apart, 15mm away from the edges. Continue to connect whole boards to the adjacent wall and into the doorway the same way as before. A skirting board will also have to be notched so the plasterboard can fit around it. Plasterboard tape should be applied to the joints of your wall to give it a smooth finish.

Fitting Cornice and Coving

When you join the top of the walls with the ceiling, you can use coving or cornice to give them a neat, decorative finish. Additionally, it is a great way of hiding any imperfections at the joints. Cornice offers a lot of options that will allow you to be quite creative. There is a wide range of cornice designs, from traditional to modern to contemporary, with the uplighting cornice becoming more and more popular in contemporary designs. As a result of this variety, you'll be able to create something that complements your home's theme or go for a new look if you're in the mood. Small changes can make a big difference, so if you need a subtle enhancement for your home, cornices and covings are fantastic options.

Trims and Moldings

Molding and trim will give your home a custom look at a low cost and make it appear upscale and well-designed. Crown molding is the most well-known of all types of molding. Baseboards are wood trim that sits on the transition between the floor and the wall.

Baseboards make a room look more beautiful but their use goes beyond just aesthetics. Some baseboards are used as a protective barrier for drywall. Depending on what type of material is used for walls, baseboards can have varying benefits.

Architectural Moldings Ideas

It is possible to achieve stunning results when you use several trim layers. The molding in this room is not limited to framing doorways and the base and top of the walls. It also frames out beams and transforms an ordinary ceiling into something spectacular. It's okay to do too much if it's done correctly.

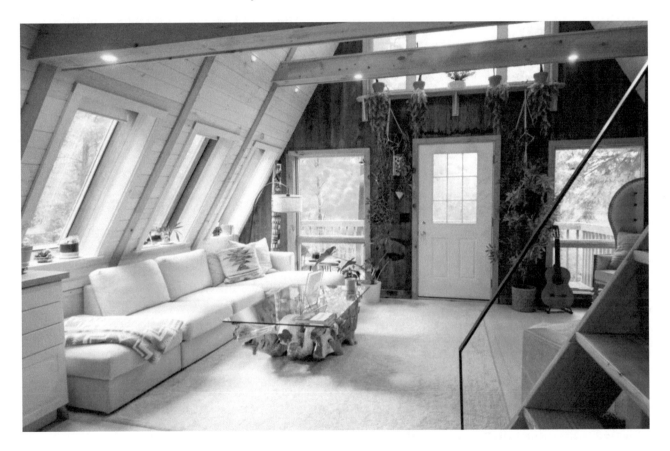

Using thin trim along the baseboards and ceiling will create a clean, contemporary look. Trim in an understated manner doesn't take up space, but instead creates the illusion of space. Paint the ceiling an off-white color to contrast the white trim—this will make the walls appear taller.

Some trim can be placed inside windows, rather than around them. To create a farmhouse-style effect, consider trimming the inside of deep-set windows. This trim not only frames the archways but also creates sophisticated paneling throughout. Any room can be jazzed up for a very low price by adding a picture frame to the wall using trim.

Fitting Arcs

Traditionally, architraves are used to frame doorways and windows. Unlike a door frame, it is primarily decorative. You can choose simple, clean architraves or elaborate, detailed ones. Architraves above doors are formally known as crossheads. They are simple, bold, and transform otherwise wasted space into something that improves a room's ceiling height. It gives the illusion of a larger doorway and makes windows seem larger. If you have windows on walls and not many pictures on the wall, you can add arcs to make windows seem larger. The effect is particularly effective for second-floor windows. You can add a splash of color to them by painting them in various colors.

Interior Paneling Ideas

When you whitewash your walls, you can keep the wood grain of the walls but remove their deep color. Once your paint is watered down, immediately wipe, then repeat until you achieve the desired color. Whitewash your paneling by mixing half-paint and half-water and applying the solution directly with a paintbrush. Prepare plenty of rags to wipe up excess water for this messy project.

It's better to not decorate your house like a cottage if you don't want wood paneling to look shabby chic. Use edgy, bohemian accents, such as dark leather furniture, pillows with patterns, and geometric lights. In addition to concealing panels, built-in bookcases can serve as a decorative backdrop. Just behind your fireplace, use wood paneling to add a touch of elegance to your walls. It will make your room stand out, making it a focal point.

Conclusion

Building a new home or renovating an existing house involves making many decisions. Some of these things might include logistics and materials. However, another big decision you will need to make is whether you will hire a designer or build it yourself. You may find that one suits you better than the other based on your lifestyle. If you want to build your own house, you should also learn how to do it. Doing it on your own has many benefits, as you will know it was done by you, and that you are proud of your finished product.

Home Repairs Never End

Maintaining your house is essential for keeping it in good condition. Always make sure the water and electricity in your house are working properly to avoid major damage. Your home could be saved from plenty of unnecessary emergencies if you pay more attention to the details. The beauty of DIY projects is that they allow you to be creative and solve problems at the same time. Simply switching to dark curtains can improve your home security since strangers will not be able to see inside.

Think Outside the Box

There are times when things go wrong and you hit roadblocks that are beyond your control. As a result of doing a lot of DIY projects, people tend to become more flexible when it comes to solving problems. Trying a new project is bound to lead to some mistakes. That's especially true when you're learning new things. Some people don't like to make mistakes or go off-plan, and this makes sense since we are taught that things must be done in a specific way to have good results. DIY projects teach you to troubleshoot and become the sort of person who can find a solution when under pressure because you will have to deal with mistakes or unknown challenges. This is a valuable life skill, no matter what your job is. The DIY-ing process is a great way to discover your strengths and talents as well as your values and passions. A DIY project lets you show off your personality.

Renovating on a Budget

In order to remodel your house on a budget, yet beautifully, it is imperative that you plan the whole process thoroughly. You need to decide how much money you are willing to spend on your house renovation in order to renovate it economically. A budget must never be overestimated. Instead, keep your budget underestimated, and then research for the things you need.

Researching your options will show you that you have a wide variety to choose from. It is also possible to buy a beautiful lamp at a cheaper price from another retailer if you like the one you saw at the high-end shop. Whenever you are renovating your home on a budget, you should remember that you can often find most of the supplies at a low price if you research and find the furniture or paint you like. Use online shopping, thrift stores, and secondhand furniture shops to make your purchases.

DIY renovations prepare you for almost anything. Getting kids, changing styles, and adding children to your family are all part of a continuous renovation process. Gaining the proper skills to maintain your home will help you prepare for a myriad of changes.

Leave a 1- Click Review

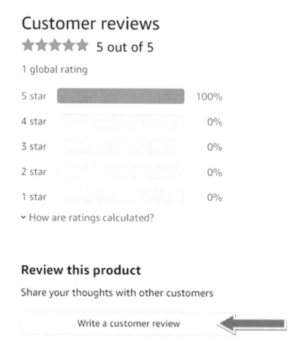

I would greatly appreciate you taking the time to write a quick review on Amazon, even a few sentences would be greatly appreciated!

References

B&Q. (2017, January 5). How to install a bar mixer shower. www.youtube.com. https://www.youtube.com/watch?v=THBH0yM5GO0

Bandon, A. (2005, October 26). The Best Techniques for Hanging Wallpaper. This Old House. https://www.thisoldhouse.com/walls/21016439/the-best-techniques-for-hanging-wallpaper

Beaty, V. (2014, August 10). 40 Brilliant DIY Shelves That Will Beautify Your Home. DIY & Crafts. https://www.diyncrafts.com/7517/home/40-brilliant-diy-shelves-will-beautify-home

Beaulieu, D. (2018, November 5). Tips for Working With Concrete. The Spruce. https://www.thespruce.com/cement-work-tips-for-working-with-concrete-2132233

Beck, A. (2021). Follow These 10 Steps to Create a Magnificent First Garden. Better Homes & Gardens. https://www.bhg.com/gardening/yard/garden-care/ten-steps-to-beginning-a-garden/

Building Construction. (2020). How To Build And Complete An Efficient And Fastest Water Storage Tank - Building Water Tanks. www.youtube.com. https://www.youtube.com/watch?v=6lBaNZkOCsg

Carmichael, J. (2018, April 27). 5 Common Questions About Concealing Surface Pipework [Boiler Relocation]. Superwarm Blog. https://www.superwarm.co.uk/5-common-questions-concealing-surface-pipework-relocating-boiler/

Clayton, J. (2021). How to Fit A Curtain Pole or Track | Advice | Jane Clayton. www.janeclayton.co.uk. https://www.janeclayton.co.uk/advice/how-to-fit-a-curtain-pole-or-track/

Cockril, M. (n.d.). Design Ideas for Repairing Broken Tile. Home Guides | SF Gate. Retrieved June 19, 2021, from https://homeguides.sfgate.com/design-ideas-repairing-broken-tile-67702.html

CommonSenseHome. (2020, February 21). How to Start a Garden – 10 Steps to Gardening for Beginners. Common Sense Home. https://commonsensehome.com/start-a-garden/

Derek. (2020, October 4). 10 Fascinating Benefits of DIY Projects. Life and My Finances. https://lifeandmyfinances.com/2020/10/10-fascinating-benefits-of-diy-projects/

Discover HomeSelfe. (2018, December 3). The Homeowners DIY Revolution: How Much are you REALLY Saving? HomeSelfe. https://www.homeselfe.com/the-homeowners-diy-revolution-how-much-are-you-really-saving/

Edwards, H. (2014, September 28). Why DIY is Good for Your Soul, Not Just Your Home. Houzz. https://www.houzz.com.au/magazine/why-diy-is-good-for-your-soul-not-just-your-home-stsetivw-vs~31502370

Edwards, M. (2012). Suspended Timber Floor and How to Build a Floating Hollow Timber Floor | DIY Doctor. DIY Doctor. https://www.diydoctor.org.uk/projects/hollowfloor.htm

Edwards, R. (2020, October 15). 10 Simple Ways to Secure Your New Home. SafeWise. https://www.safewise.com/blog/10-simple-ways-to-secure-your-new-home/

Eileen. (2018, January 7). How to Find Time for DIY Projects | Ways to Make Time in a Busy Day. Just Measuring Up. https://www.justmeasuringup.com/find-diy-time/

Electrical Safety First. (n.d.). Overloading Sockets. Electrical Safety First. https://www.electricalsafetyfirst.org.uk/guidance/safety-around-the-home/overloading-sockets/

Engel, A. (2020, December 4). What to Know About Cutting Stair Stringers. This Old House. https://www.thisoldhouse.com/stairs/21591423/how-to-cut-stair-stringers

Family Handyman. (n.d.-a). DIY Furnace Maintenance Will Save A Repair Bill. Family Handyman. Retrieved June 25, 2021, from https://www.familyhandyman.com/project/do-it-yourself-furnace-maintenance-will-save-a-repair-bill/

Family Handyman. (n.d.-b). Install an In-Ground Drainage System. Family Handyman. Retrieved June 21, 2021, from https://www.familyhandyman.com/project/install-an-in-ground-drainage-system/

Flaherty, E. (2019, July 23). 18 DIY Fixes for Broken Electrical Items at Home. Family Handyman. https://www.familyhandyman.com/list/fixes-for-broken-electrical-fixtures/

Frederick, L. (2009). 10 Things You Must Know: Accent Lighting. DIY. https://www.diynetwork.com/how-to/make-and-decorate/decorating/10-things-you-must-know-accent-lighting

Gapp, O. (2019, November 25). 5 Benefits of DIY Projects for Your Home - Louie's Ace Hardware. https://louieshomecenter.com/2019/11/5-benefits-of-diy-projects-for-your-home/

Garcia, I. (2020, February 20). Creative DIY Curtains. House Beautiful. https://www.housebeautiful.com/lifestyle/g30896430/diy-curtains/?slide=2

Gardner, C. (2012, May 4). 10 DIY Pipe Fitting Projects (No Plumbing Required). Bob Vila. https://www.bobvila.com/articles/diy-pipe-fitting-projects/

Geerts, S. (2020, May 21). 13 Things to Know Before You Build a Fence. Better Homes & Gardens. https://www.bhg.com/home-improvement/outdoor/fences/before-you-build-a-fence/

Geiger, C. (2020, April 30). How to Get Rid of Black Mold for Good. Country Living. https://www.countryliving.com/home-maintenance/cleaning/a27379221/black-mold-removal/

Gilbert, N. (2020, February 9). How to Refinish Worn Out Stair Treads. This Old House. https://www.thisoldhouse.com/stairs/21122989/how-to-refinish-worn-out-stair-treads

Gold, J. (2019, May 29). DIY Vs. Pro -- Who's Doing What At Home? Forbes. https://www.forbes.com/sites/jamiegold/2019/05/29/diy-vs-pro-whos-doing-what-at-home/?sh=3ebc64e17b15

Handyman Magazine. (n.d.). How to Solder Copper Pipe Joints. Family Handyman. Retrieved June 21, 2021, from https://www.familyhandyman.com/project/how-to-solder-copper-pipe-joints/

Hatcher, V. (2020, September 14). Importance Of Maintaining Drain, Waste, And Vent Plumbing In Buildings. Facility Executive - Creating Intelligent Buildings. https://facilityexecutive.com/2020/09/importance-of-maintaining-drain-waste-and-vent-systems-in-buildings/

Heinz, A. (2019, July 11). 10 Household Bugs and Natural Remedies For Ridding Them | ApartmentGuide.com. Apartment Living Tips - Apartment Tips from ApartmentGuide.com. https://www.apartmentguide.com/blog/house-bugs/

Herman, K. (2021, February 23). Here's How To Hang Anything And Everything On Your Walls. BuzzFeed. https://www.buzzfeed.com/katyherman/heres-how-to-hang-anything-and-everything-on-your-walls

Home Hardware. (2020, October 13). Fixing a Leaking tap. Home Hardware. https://www.homehardware.com.au/diy-ideas-advice/fixing-a-leaking-tap/

Home Improvement. (n.d.). How to Build a Shower Enclosure for Your DIY Bathroom Remodel. Better Homes & Gardens. Retrieved June 21, 2021, from https://www.bhg.com/home-improvement/plumbing/how-to-build-a-shower-enclosure/

Home RenoVision DIY. (2020, July 26). All You Need To Know About Flooring Options. www.youtube.com. https://www.youtube.com/watch?v=i-LAnShDPZc

Image 1: From Unsplash, by Jane Palash, 2019 https://unsplash.com/photos/83EEDevoNls Copyright 2019, by Jane Palash, Unsplash

Image 2: From Unsplash, by Annie Gray, 2017 https://unsplash.com/photos/WEWTGkPUVTo Copyright 2017, by Annie Gray, Unsplash

Image 3: From Unsplash, by Louis Hansel-Restaurant Photographer, 2019 https://unsplash.com/photos/Rf9eElW3Qxo Copyright 2019, by Louis Hansel-Restaurant Photographer, Unsplash

Image 4: From Pixabay, by Michal Jarmoluk , 2013 https://pixabay.com/photos/electrician-repair-electricity-1080554/ Copyright 2013, by Michal Jarmoluk, Pixabay

Image 5: From Unsplash, by Outside Co, 2017 https://unsplash.com/photos/R-LK3sqLiBw Copyright 2017, by Outside Co, Unsplash

Image 6: From Vecteezy, by pisit_tar676462, 2021 https://www.vecteezy.com/photo/1884363-colorful-rolls-of-wallpaper Copyright 2021, by pisit_tar676462, Vecteezy

Image 7: From Freepik, by Volodymyr, 2020 https://www.freepik.com/premium-photo/man-putting-wallpaper-home_9272194.htm#page=1&query=applying%20wallpaper&position=3 Copyright 2020, by Volodymyr, Freepik

Image 8:From Vecteezy, by pisit_tar676462, 2021

https://www.vecteezy.com/photo/1903928-close-up-of-a-curtain Copyright 2021, by pisit_tar676462, Vecteezy

Image 9:From Vecteezy, by khuntuu1973351526, 2019

https://www.vecteezy.com/photo/2463361-close-up-on-many-stacking-carpet-rolls Copyright 2019, by khuntuu1973351526, Vecteezy

Image 10: From Unsplash, by HausPhotoMedia, 2019

https://unsplash.com/photos/aRT5UCf2MYY Copyright 2019, by HausPhotoMedia, Unsplash

Image 11:From Pixabay, by SatyaPrem, 2018 https://pixabay.com/photos/architecture-roof-terrace-flat-roof-3662619/ Copyright 2018, by SatyaPrem, Pixabay

Image 12:From Pixabay, by sueha, 2020 https://pixabay.com/photos/cordes-sur-ciel-france-south-west-4879397/ Copyright 2020, by sueha, Pixabay

Image 13:From Freepik, by Jcomp, n.d. https://www.freepik.com/free-photo/carpenter-holds-glue-attaches-window_8971454.htm#page=1&query=home%20window%20repair&position=5 Copyright n.d., by Jcomp, Freepik

Image 14:From Vecteezy, by advenshotlife464657, 2018

https://www.vecteezy.com/photo/2746936-texture-white-wooden-shutters Copyright 2018, by advenshotlife464657, Vecteezy

Image 15:From Vecteezy, by peterspiro, 2009 https://www.vecteezy.com/photo/958134-tudor-style-house-entrance Copyright 2009, by peterspiro, Vecteezy

Image 16: From Freepik, by Drinkins, 2020 https://www.freepik.com/premium-photo/man-clamps-loose-screw-with-electric-screwdriver_9373308.htm#page=1&query=loose%20door%20handle&position=0 Copyright 2020, by Drinkins, Freepik

Image 17: From Vecteezy, by stevanovicigor, 2015 https://www.vecteezy.com/photo/1103670-copper-pipes Copyright 2015, by stevanovicigor, Vecteezy

Image 18: From Vecteezy, by ukrainec, 2015 https://www.vecteezy.com/photo/1106848-plumbing-tools-on-the-kitchen Copyright 2015, by ukrainec, Vecteezy

Image 19: From Vecteezy, by idmanjoe, 2014 https://www.vecteezy.com/photo/1115967-pvc-water-pipe Copyright 2014, by idmanjoe, Vecteezy

Image 20: From Unsplash, by Doug Greenman, 2020 https://unsplash.com/photos/4ljbuB52IPQ Copyright 2020, by Doug Greenman, Unsplash

Image 21: From Pixabay, by Eugene_Brennan, 2015 https://pixabay.com/photos/plumbing-fittings-pipe-connection-1002142/ Copyright 2015, by Eugene_Brennan, Pixabay

Image 22: From Vecteezy, by pikyarm108, 2015 https://www.vecteezy.com/photo/902545-kid-washing-hands-with-mother-selective-focus-point Copyright 2015, by pikyarm108, Vecteezy

Image 23: From Freepik, by Wirestock, 2021 https://www.freepik.com/free-photo/plumbing-repair-service_12152405.htm#page=1&query=fixing%20taps&position=1 Copyright 2021, by Wirestock, Freepik

Image 24: From Freepik, by Andranik, 2021 https://www.freepik.com/premium-photo/man-repair-fixing-shower-faucet-bathroom_15469815.htm#page=1&query=installing%20a%20shower&position=2 Copyright 2021, by Andranik, Freepik

Image 25: From Vecteezy, by pisit_tar676462, 2021 https://www.vecteezy.com/photo/2010164-white-towels-on-the-bathtub Copyright 2021, by pisit_tar676462, Vecteezy

Image 26: From Freepik, by Diana, 2020 https://www.freepik.com/free-photo/close-view-young-worker-laying-floor-with-laminated-flooring-boards_9695804.htm#page=1&query=laying%20wood%20floors&position=2 Copyright 2020, y Diana, Freepik

Image 27: From Vecteezy, by andriymedvediuk, 2015 https://www.vecteezy.com/photo/2254794-stairs-and-carpet-inside-a-newly-modernized-house-interior-hallway-with-stairs Copyright 2015, by andriymedvediuk, Vecteezy

Image 28: From Freepik, by Ungvar, 2019 https://www.freepik.com/premium-photo/how-install-stair-railing-kit-installation-wooden_3905892.htm#page=1&query=new%20house%20handrail&position=29 Copyright 2019, by Ungvar, Freepik

Image 29: From Freepik, by Etaphop, 2018 https://www.freepik.com/premium-photo/electrician-is-using-digital-meter-measure-voltage-power-outlet_2979205.htm#page=1&query=measuring%20voltage%20at%20home&position=16 Copyright 2018, by Etaphop, Freepik

Image 30: From Vecteezy, by henfaes, 2015 https://www.vecteezy.com/photo/870496-electrician-wiring-a-new-circuit-breaker-for-a-residential-property Copyright 2015, by henfaes, Vecteezy

Image 31: From Unsplash, by Le Creuset 2019
https://unsplash.com/photos/m4ChAAL8E98?utm_source=unsplash&utm_medium=referral&utm_content=creditShareLink Copyright 2019, by Le Creuset, Unsplash

Image 32: From Vecteezy, by Marko Klaric, 2016
https://www.vecteezy.com/photo/2074263-interior-with-a-chalkboard-mockup-in-3d-illustration Copyright 2016, by Marko_Klaric, Vecteezy

Image 33:From Pixabay, by 3844328, 2016 https://pixabay.com/photos/wireless-home-router-adsl-modem-1861612/ Copyright 2016, by 3844328, Pixabay

Image 34: From Unsplash, by Ýlona María Rybka 2019
https://unsplash.com/photos/TAUybipul4Q Copyright 2019, by Ýlona María Rybka, Unsplash

Image 35: From Vecteezy, by Macrovector, 2021 https://www.vecteezy.com/vector-art/2908519-colored-realistic-water-heater-boiler-composition-vector-illustration Copyright 2021, by Macrovector, Vecteezy

Image 36: From Freepik, by Prostooleh, 2020 https://www.freepik.com/free-photo/family-works-garden-near-house_9344675.htm#page=1&query=house%20vegetable%20garden&position=45#position=45&page=1&query=house%20vegetable%20garden Copyright 2020, by Prostooleh, Freepik

Image 37: From Unsplash, by David Griffiths 2021
https://unsplash.com/photos/lHTIvZFyuh4 Copyright 2021, by David Griffiths, Unsplash

Image 38: From Vecteezy, by kevenodes 2020 https://www.vecteezy.com/vector-art/113509-stok-vector-bricklayer Copyright 2020, by kevenodes, Vecteezy

Image 39: From Vecteezy, by eyjafjallajokull 2014
https://www.vecteezy.com/photo/873499-worker-paving-new-sidewalk-3 Copyright 2014, by eyjafjallajokull, Vecteezy

Image 40: From Vecteezy, by studio2013 2000 https://www.vecteezy.com/photo/1960330-stepping-stones-in-garden Copyright 2000, by studio2013, Vecteezy

Image 41: From Vecteezy, by philippe60255 2008
https://www.vecteezy.com/photo/2979961-small-stone-pond-with-aquatic-plants-in-a-garden-in-portugal Copyright 2008, by philippe60255, Vecteezy

Image 42: From Freepik, by Bilanol, 2020 https://www.freepik.com/premium-photo/worker-protective-respirator-mask-insulating-rock-wool-insulation-wooden-frame-future-house-walls-cold-barrier_6494551.htm?query=insulating%20walls Copyright 2020, by Bilanon, Freepik

Image 43: From Unsplash, by Andrea Davis, 2020
https://unsplash.com/photos/IWfe63thJxk Copyright 2020, by Andrea Davis, Unsplash

Image 44: From Freepik, by Ijeab, 2017 https://www.freepik.com/free-photo/graphic-design-color-swatches-pens-desk-architectural-drawing-with-work-tools-accessories_1235465.htm#page=1&query=interior%20design&position=20 Copyright 2017, by Ijeab, Freepik

Karen. (2020, August 25). How to Build Interior Window Shutters. The Art of Doing Stuff. https://www.theartofdoingstuff.com/how-to-build-interior-shutters/

Kruger, E. (2015, March 20). 30 Magnificent DIY Rugs to Brighten up Your Home. DIY & Crafts. https://www.diyncrafts.com/11077/home/30-magnificent-diy-rugs-to-brighten-up-your-home

Lissack, M. (2017, June 29). How To Put Up Wallpaper: A Simple & Easy Guide. MELANIE LISSACK INTERIORS. https://www.melanielissackinteriors.com/blog/2017/6/26/how-to-wallpaper-a-simple-easy-guide

Lumber, D. (2015, September 8). How-To: DIY Basics. www.youtube.com. https://www.youtube.com/watch?v=JQ61gpnYxNU

Lynch, A. (2016, July 15). Weekend Projects: 5 Designs for a DIY Door. Bob Vila. https://www.bobvila.com/articles/how-to-build-a-door/

Marshalls. (2011, September 4). How to Build a Garden Wall 2019 | MarshallsTV. www.youtube.com. https://www.youtube.com/watch?v=IzM23fh8h98

McCollum, N. (2019, December 9). 5 Common Construction Laws You Should Know Before You Build. This Old House. https://www.thisoldhouse.com/home-finances/21097121/5-common-construction-laws-you-should-know-before-you-build

Mitre 10 New Zealand. (2020, November 25). How to Install a Small Water Tank | Mitre 10 Easy As DIY. www.youtube.com. https://www.youtube.com/watch?v=pxm1jkxlhB8

MrFixIt DIY. (2019, September 27). How to Install a Bathroom Faucet | A DIY Guide. www.youtube.com. https://www.youtube.com/watch?v=vpq_jFyf8Yo

Mueller, L. (2019, March 29). 16 Super Easy DIY Home Improvement Ideas. Moving.com. https://www.moving.com/tips/16-super-easy-diy-home-improvement-ideas/

Ngo, D. (2020, April 30). Home Wi-Fi Network Explained: How to Fully Build One 100% from Scratch | Dong Knows Tech. Dongknows.com. https://dongknows.com/home-wi-fi-router-setup/

Pick, C. (2019, December 14). Can I Install My Own Electric Cooker? Chef's Pick. https://chefspick.co.uk/can-i-install-my-own-electric-cooker/

Plumbcare.com. (n.d.). Blog | Basic plumbing skills everyone should have. www.plumbcare.com. Retrieved June 16, 2021, from https://www.plumbcare.com/blog/2020/01/basic-plumbing-skills-everyone-should-have

Plumbworld. (2019, July 26). What Are The Different Types of Showers? Plumbworld. https://www.plumbworld.co.uk/blog/what-are-the-different-types-of-shower

Raymond, D. (2011, November 14). How to Replace a Baluster. This Old House. https://www.thisoldhouse.com/stairs/21016512/how-to-replace-a-baluster

Red Carpet Service. (2017, May). Best Home Remedies To Clear A Drain Clog | General Plumbing. General Plumbing and Air Conditioning. https://www.generalplumbing.com/blog/2017/may/home-remedies-for-a-clogged-drain/

Ridenour, E. (2020, March 17). 10 Ways to Insulate Your Home Without Opening Up Walls. Family Handyman. https://www.familyhandyman.com/list/10-ways-to-insulate-your-home-without-opening-up-walls/

Riha, J. (n.d.). What You Need to Know Before Starting a Floor Installation. DIY. Retrieved June 22, 2021, from https://www.diynetwork.com/how-to/rooms-and-spaces/floors/what-you-need-to-know-before-starting-a-floor-installation

Rudd, L. (2017, October 9). Diagnose central heating problems | How-to videos, DIY as well as Lifestyle tips and tricks. Living - Your Home, DIY and Life by HomeServe. https://www.homeserve.com/uk/living/how-to/diagnose-central-heating-problems/

Sawyer, A. (2018, August 20). 5 Tricks to Hanging Blinds Perfectly the First Time. The House Designers. https://www.thehousedesigners.com/blog/5-tricks-to-hanging-blinds-perfectly-the-first-time/

Silverline Tools. (2014). How To Build & Lay Timber Decking [YouTube Video]. In YouTube. https://www.youtube.com/watch?v=Ul5HVbri5Nw

Sims, M. (2019, December 16). Common Issues When Renovating a Home and How to Prepare. www.simsbuilders.com. https://www.simsbuilders.com/blog/common-issues-renovating-home-prepare

Sobieski Plumbing. (2019, October 4). What is a Drain-Waste-Vent (DWV) System? Sobieski Services | DE, NJ, PA, MD. https://www.sobieskiinc.com/blog/what-is-drain-waste-vent-dwv-system/

Step by Step Guide: How to Build a Stud Wall. (2020, June 4). Saxton Blades Blog. https://www.saxtonblades.co.uk/blog/step-by-step-guide-how-to-build-a-stud-wall/

TGG. (2017, May 14). Gorgeous DIY Garden Gate Ideas & Projects • The Garden Glove. The Garden Glove. https://www.thegardenglove.com/diy-gorgeous-garden-gates/

The Home Depot. (2019). Bathtub Replacement | How to Install a Bathtub | The Home Depot. www.youtube.com. https://www.youtube.com/watch?v=wo1Uv2vlMO8

The Home Depot. (2021, June 1). How To Build a Water Garden | The Home Depot. www.youtube.com. https://www.youtube.com/watch?v=qUk5XgsEdg8

TheRoofWindowStore. (2020). How to Clean Your Roof Windows. Theroofwindowstore.co.uk. https://theroofwindowstore.co.uk/blog-articles/how-to-clean-your-roof-window?consent=none&ref-original=https%3A%2F%2Fwww.google.com%2F

Van Graan, J. (2019, March 28). 8 things to consider before renovating your home | homify. Homify.co.za. https://www.homify.co.za/ideabooks/6522704/8-things-to-consider-before-renovating-your-home

Wallender, L. (2008, June 25). 7 Basic Types of Plumbing Pipes You Might Encounter. The
Spruce; TheSpruce. https://www.thespruce.com/basic-types-of-plumbing-pipes-
1822487

Yamada, K. (2014, November 12). Beginner's Electronics: 10 Skills You Need to Know.
MUO. https://www.makeuseof.com/tag/beginners-electronics-10-skills-you-need-to-
know/

Young, E. (2021, May 11). 10 Best Living Room Shelving Ideas. Family Handyman.
https://www.familyhandyman.com/list/living-room-shelving-ideas/

Made in the USA
Columbia, SC
12 December 2023

27825635R10087